"Singin' a Lonesome Song"

Texas Prison Tales

Gary Brown

Republic of Texas Press
Plano, Texas

Library of Congress Cataloging-in-Publication Data

Brown, Gary., 1945-
    Singin' a lonesome song : Texas prison tales / Gary Brown.
        p. cm.
    Includes bibliographical references and index.
    ISBN 1-55622-845-7 (pbk.)
    1. Prisoners—Texas—Biography. I. Title.

HV8657.B76 2000
365'.6'092—dc21   00-051713
[B]   CIP

© 2001, Gary Brown
All Rights Reserved

Republic of Texas Press is an imprint of Wordware Publishing, Inc.
No part of this book may be reproduced in any form or by
any means without permission in writing from
Wordware Publishing, Inc.

Printed in the United States of America

ISBN 1-55622-845-7
10 9 8 7 6 5 4 3 2 1
0012

All inquiries for volume purchases of this book should be addressed to
Wordware Publishing, Inc., at 2320 Los Rios Boulevard, Plano, Texas 75074.
Telephone inquiries may be made by calling:

(972) 423-0090

Dedication

This book is dedicated to

Spence Watkins
1951-1998

A good friend and professional educator
who made a difference in the Texas prison system.

Contents

Contents

Preface

I walked onto the Ramsey I Unit of the Texas Department of Corrections for the first time on the evening of January 12, 1976. Nothing in my orientation as a prison college teacher had prepared me for what I encountered.

When I walked off the Jester III Unit on September 15, 1999, I realized that during the interim twenty-three years I had worked as a teacher and counselor I had learned a great deal.

During those years I had watched the Texas prison system grow from 23,000 inmates in 16 units to over 143,500 inmates in over 120 prison units. I had seen a self-supporting agricultural-based prison system develop into a multimillion-dollar correctional industry that had become a microcosm of society itself with industries, schools, hospitals, and almost every other aspect of a "free society."

The Texas Department of Criminal Justice agency I retired from in 1999 was basically unrecognizable from the Texas Department of Corrections I had first entered at Ramsey I in 1976.

Those twenty-three years I worked in Texas prisons also brought what sometimes seemed an endless cycle of charges of corruption, brutality, and inefficiency. Construction deals were investigated, food substitute contracts were challenged, and charges of brutality led to several guards and high-ranking security officers leaving the agency over those years.

But as I learned more about the history of the 150-year-old Texas prison system and the inmates and convicts who have been incarcerated in it, I realized that very little new had happened between 1976 and 1999 that hadn't already happened before.

I learned that the federal judge condemning the Texas prison system in the 1980s was not a judicial first; a city judge had condemned the conditions in the Houston city jail as early as 1838.

I came to realize that while private prisons are a controversial correctional issue today, the convict lease system rented out inmates to private industry from 1871 to 1909 with terrible incidents of cruelty and abuse.

Today the TDCJ budget has a line item of over $53 million to provide educational opportunities for inmates and touts it as a "model." In fact, the Texas prison system first provided for inmate education in 1895, but unfortunately the legislature didn't get around to funding the program until 1911. Inmate education in some form has existed since that time.

In the 1980s overcrowding forced early releases and caused backlogs in county jails. In 1930 an inmate named Clyde Barrow was housed in county jail nearly a year because the Huntsville Unit was over capacity and no new inmates were being accepted.

During Thanksgiving of 1998 seven inmates attempted to escape Death Row: one succeeded in climbing over the fence only to die in the Trinity River nearby. In 1934 six inmates attempted to escape the Death House; three made it over the brick walls in Huntsville and claim the only successful escape from the death chamber.

Increasingly the Texas prison system is housing serial or multiple-murder criminals, yet these modern-day killers pale in comparison to another inmate in the 1800s named John Wesley Hardin.

Recently the Texas death penalty by lethal injection has come under heavy criticism. But as far back as 1924 it was criticism of county hanging practices that led to Texas adopting the electric chair. Then, a half-century after that, "Old Sparky" would be declared "cruel and unusual punishment" and abolished in favor of lethal injection.

As much as today's Texas prison administration would like to portray itself as progressive and modern, the fact remains that the story of Texas's prisons is not one of progress but of cycles. What goes around comes around.

Yes, when I walked off the Jester III Unit on September 15, 1999, I realized that during those interim twenty-three years working as a teacher and counselor I had indeed learned a great deal. But in reality, I hadn't seen anything new.

Singin' a Lonesome Song is not a book about the Texas prison system itself. It is not a textbook about crime, criminology, penology, or correctional theory.

It is a book about convicts and inmates who have made the Texas prison system the most colorful in the world over the past 150 years.

It is about a gunslinger from the 1800s and a burlesque stripper from the 1950s. It is about a Kiowa Indian chief, a blues musician, several gangsters, an escape artist, the "meanest man in Texas," and a Mexican vaquero riding a *yegua trigueña* across Texas only to become an inmate barber at Huntsville.

Singin' a Lonesome Song is about chain-bus drivers, wild bull riders, and a prison baseball team that took on the Texas semi-pro champions in Houston's old Buff Stadium.

It is about the morbid history of Old Sparky and the final moments leading up to the electrocution of two of Texas's most notorious gangsters.

It is a book about inmates and prisoners of war supplying materials to the Confederate army, about convict laborers building a state railroad and quarrying the marble that built our beautiful capitol building in Austin.

The stories are true but sometimes hard to believe. They include an inmate who escaped Huntsville to visit Governor Miriam Ferguson in her office and ask for a pardon, a bizarre game of "musical chairs" involving the electric chair, and an inmate so violent he was welded into an abandoned morgue building at Huntsville.

The Texas prison stories include virtually every segment of society. Among the participants are black, white, and Mexican inmates and a Native American tribal chief. Men and women both have impacted the prison system over the years, as have Texans from the lowest and highest echelons of the state.

Combined, they have made the Texas prison system story one of color, sadness, happiness, hope, despair, and every other emotion incarcerated people can experience from behind bars that separate them from freedom.

They are the true voices of *Singin' a Lonesome Song*.

Chapter One

"Texas Convict #7109"— John Wesley Hardin

When the heavily guarded wagon entered the Huntsville prison compound on October 5, 1878, the other convicts stopped what they were doing and stood around staring—concentrating particularly on one of the newly arrived inmates.

At five feet nine inches and one hundred sixty pounds, the new convict was not a particularly imposing figure. Despite his filthy, tattered jailhouse traveling clothes, it was obvious he was a handsome man. He had dirty brown hair and a mustache with some facial growth. Only one feature of this man betrayed his deadly past. It was often reported during his lifetime that his cold, piercing eyes flashed warning or danger to all who saw him up close.

There was good reason for that feeling of warning or danger. Texas Convict #7109 in the Huntsville prison compound that morning, beginning a twenty-five-year sentence, was none other than the infamous John Wesley Hardin. Depending on who was doing the counting, this convict had killed between forty-two and fifty-one men by the time he reached prison in Texas.

Despite the relatively small stature of this new arrival, those convicts in the prison yard who stopped to watch probably harbored no illusions of taking advantage of this new inmate. John Wesley Hardin was no serial killer of women, children, or weak men.

To the contrary, Hardin (he referred to himself as "Wes") killed his armed opponents in face-to-face contests. Many people thought in 1878—and many historians feel today—that of all the men John Wesley shot down, only one could have been considered pure murder by the laws of the time in which he lived. Of the forty-two documented killings attributed to him, all but that one would have been considered a fair fight. Many casualties were men of poor judgement who had come looking for him.

And the continuing rumor that he once shot a man for snoring too loud was just that—one of the many rumors that have been attributed to this man who entered the Texas prison system in October of 1878.

In a routine that continues today in Texas prisons, Hardin was processed into the prison system by being stripped, given a shave and haircut, and a physical inventory of body markings recorded.

We have today a personal record of this inmate's time in prison. John Wesley Hardin kept a diary while he was incarcerated and included this chapter in what would become his autobiography published after his death as *The Life of John Wesley Hardin As Written by Himself.*[1]

Hardin recorded that he was given a breakfast of coffee, bacon, bread, and molasses that morning. Prison records indicate that he was shaved and showered before his physical inventory was taken. He was listed as having dark hair, hazel eyes, and a light complexion. The inspection of his body revealed wounds and scars over virtually every part of his body—one vestige of the life he had led during his short twenty-six years. He was then given a work assignment in the wheelwright shop at the Huntsville unit.

But as notorious as Hardin was in 1878, the novelty of his arrival in prison soon wore off as the other convicts returned to their daily routines. The Texas prison system had a reputation in 1878 as being a tough place to do time, and to the hardened convicts there, Hardin was probably just another badman who had fallen on hard times.

One week after his arrival a convict jumped to his death from the second story hospital at the unit. He was Chief Satanta—the once feared and hated Kiowa leader sentenced to life for murders committed in North Texas during the plains wars. Rumors swept the prison that he had been pushed from the window and murdered; other rumors claimed he had committed suicide rather than die in captivity. But almost immediately after his arrival at Huntsville, Wes Hardin was no longer the chief topic of discussion among the inmates.

Which must have suited him fine since he had already started scheming to escape from prison.

With surprising candor, Hardin later wrote of his own naivete while incarcerated. Again and again, starting with his time in county jails before prison induction, he confided in and relied upon fellow inmates only to be betrayed to officials. In his autobiography he wrote, "I knew there were a heap of Judases and Benedict Arnolds in the world and had had a life-long experience with the meaning of the word treachery. I believed, however, that in jail even a coward was a brave man, so I went to work to plan my escape."

Violating virtually every rule of escape planning, Hardin incorporated an unbelievable seventy-five inmates in a plan to tunnel from the wheelwright shop some seventy-five yards to the prison armory. Hardin then envisioned the inmates seizing the guard's guns, taking control of the prison, and freeing all the prisoners (except the "rape fiends").

The plan started around November 1, 1878—some three weeks after his arrival—and was completed around the twentieth. According to Hardin, all that was left was to burst through the pine wood floor of the armory while the unarmed guards were eating supper and execute the escape plan. At this point he had his first experience with prison "snitches."

The plan was exposed by other inmates, and Hardin and nine other convicts were seized. A ball and chain was forged onto his ankle, and he was thrown into a darkened solitary confinement cell and fed bread and water for fifteen days. Even worse, Hardin was now tabbed by prison officials as an escape risk and would be watched even closer and punished more severely because of it. The heavy steel ball chained to his ankle would remain after his release from solitary.

Considering the threat to prison officials and guards and the near completion of the scheme, Hardin was probably lucky to get off as easily as he did this time. The two weeks in solitary on bread and water did not, however, deter his drive to escape from prison.

After release from solitary, Hardin was celled with a lifer working in the cellblock as a "turnkey." Turnkeys served prison officials in a manner much like the later infamous and hated "building tenders." They were inmates who were given special privileges for controlling the behavior of the general inmate population. In short, they were "inmate guards."

Hardin's cellmate was responsible for controlling and monitoring the movement of inmates through the use of a gate key. Despite the fact the turnkey had been involved in the escape plan and had received a privileged job rather than punishment, Hardin failed to recognize that his cellmate was now working for the authorities as a snitch.

Recognizing the advantage of having an accomplice with access to prison keys, Hardin immediately enlisted his cellmate to begin duplicating keys to other cells, riot gates, and even the prison exits. He even obtained a key that allowed him to remove the ball-and-chain shackles at night.

His plan was to escape on the evening of December 26 by releasing the other convicts in his cellblock and then, in the ensuing confusion and alarm, use the keys to open bars, gates, and finally one of the exit doors to the prison. He had, he later claimed, two pistols that had been smuggled into the prison by a trusty.

As in the tunneling scheme, he was "snitched off"—this time by his turnkey cellmate. And this time the prison officials were not as lenient with him.

The night of the planned escape, prison guards entered his cell, found the keys, and bound his hands and feet with four lengths of rope. They forced him face-down on the concrete floor using the ropes to hold him "spread-eagled" and stripped his clothes. Then, using a strap consisting of four thick strands of harness leather, they gave him the maximum thirty-nine lashes allowed by prison regulations at that time.

With 156 raw welts on his back, sides, and legs, Hardin was then taken to a darkened solitary cell and, according to his account, left for three days without food or water. On the fourth day he was carried to another cell "in a high fever" and left for another thirty days.

It was now February of 1879, and John Wesley Hardin had been in prison less than four months. On February 9 he wrote his wife that he was going to obey orders and "do right." It appears that prison officials had, as they still refer to it, "gotten his heart right."

On the first of February he was assigned to work in the prison carpentry shop, but he claims he successfully used his flogging injuries to avoid work most of the time. By June he had been transferred to the boot and shoe shop—a job he held until 1883.

If Hardin had professed to having his heart right in February, by the summer of 1879 he had had a "change of heart" and was once again scheming to escape from Huntsville. By January of 1880 reports indicated that he was one of four inmates captured trying to escape again. This time, no longer trusting the other convicts who had always betrayed him, Hardin relied on one other inmate and concentrated on bribing a guard. Again, he was snitched off, thrown into solitary, and flogged although by his own account "not so cruelly as before."

Hardin would later claim he was flogged a third time—"for an imaginary crime"—as a scare tactic. It must have worked, since from that time John Wesley Hardin appears to have become a model prisoner.

He did later claim involvement in one last escape plan involving the smuggling of guns into the prison—involvement that he claims he withdrew from just before the scheme was disclosed by other inmates. The plan was executed and failed and those involved flogged by the guards. Hardin was excused from punishment despite his involvement in the planning of the escape—which included the contingency of killing guards if necessary. Given his past history of escape attempts and the vengeful position prison officials took towards such inmates, this leniency was curious.

Upon arrival at Huntsville, prison officials had listed his education as "common," which probably set him far above the educational levels of the majority of convicts in prison in Texas at the time. His father had been a lawyer, schoolteacher, and Methodist minister, and it can probably be assumed that Wes Hardin could at least read and write by the time he entered prison.

Hardin claimed it was during his prison years that he began reading extensively and developed an interest in mathematics. During the years of 1880, 1881, and 1882 he was reported to be the president of a debating society at Huntsville, and completely out of character for the most notorious gunman in Texas at that time, he had become the superintendent of the inmate Sunday school class. His father being a Methodist minister and he, himself, having been named for the founder of Methodism, it is certain he had received some level of religious instruction as a child.

Prison records indicate Wes Hardin's body showed the scars from various wounds upon his arrival at Huntsville. In the fall of 1883 one of those old wounds, a shotgun wound in his side and stomach, abscessed. He later claimed that prison officials "made fun of me and treated me cruelly" while refusing him a hospital bed. In part due to his suffering but also in reaction to his lack of treatment, Hardin lay in his cell for eight months recuperating. Finally prison officials got tired of his inactivity and put him on a bread and water diet until he agreed to return to work.

He was assigned to the tailor shop making quilts. It remains difficult to visualize the man once considered the most dangerous gunslinger in the West at a quilting frame in the Texas prison shop, but it appears to have been a job assignment that was favorable to both the prison system and Wes Hardin.

Hardin later reported that his work supervisor there allowed him to read during lulls in the work schedule and that he had now become a "constant reader." Still, his health was failing and as late as September 12, 1884, the *Laredo Times* reported him "close to death."

It had become apparent that, for some time, Wes Hardin was no longer the same feared killer he had been on that October 5, 1878 day when he had entered the Huntsville prison compound. In fact, he may have become vulnerable.

Leon Metz, in his 1966 book *John Wesley Hardin, Dark Angel of Texas*[2], speculates that Hardin may have been involved in, or possibly coerced into, a series of compromising acts while at Huntsville. Citing correspondence by Hardin during this period, Metz quotes phrases such as "not on account of any unfaithfulness on my part" and "disgraceful correspondence and something I cannot mention now." Metz suggests that his behavior humiliated and disgraced Hardin and that he later revealed "self-hate" because of it.[3]

Prison records do not confirm any such relationships or actions on the part of Hardin during his incarceration, and the outlaw himself makes no allusion to such incidents in his autobiography. But there could be no question that confinement at Huntsville had reduced the West's most notorious gunman to just another inmate trying to survive, do his time, and get out of prison.

The year 1885 was particularly difficult for John Wesley Hardin. On June 6 his mother passed away, and he continued to struggle with health problems. On August 26 he wrote the assistant warden a letter begging for medical attention, which appears to have resulted in his getting at least some level of treatment, and his health slowly improved.

The passing of his mother and his close brush with death seem to have focused Wes Hardin's attention on completing his twenty-five-year sentence and being discharged from prison. It was also during 1885 that he first approached the prison superintendent, Thomas Goree, for advice regarding a course of reading to prepare him to practice law.

Hardin then appears to have directed his efforts solely at obtaining a legitimate release from Texas prison. His correspondence with outside officials picked up, and in 1888 he wrote the assistant superintendent of the prison system a letter requesting a release date. The answer was curt and noncommittal: "You continue to behave yourself, and you will go out at the proper time."

In 1889 he wrote the Texas Legislature, suggesting prison reforms and changes in the sentencing laws, and he began campaigning in earnest for an early pardon or parole.

The election of 1891 resulted in a change in the Texas governor's office that Hardin felt might be favorable to his pleas for a pardon. Governor James S. Hogg quickly became the target of Hardin's letters and the petitions of others on his behalf.

Hardin's attorney back in Gonzales, Texas, however was concerned about the possibility that Wes Hardin might be released from prison only to face multiple charges in any of several counties where he had previously killed men. Such charges, the resulting trials and confinement, and possibility of resentencing to prison would negate any advantage of an early parole or pardon for Hardin's current prison sentence.

While petitions for Hardin's release flooded the governor's office, his attorney investigated and found that only DeWitt County had charges pending against his client. On January 1, 1892, Hardin accepted a two-year manslaughter sentence for a nearly two-decades-old shooting. The sentence was to run concurrent with his present prison term, meaning he would have no charges pending against him if he paroled early or was given a pardon. Because of the second sentence, the Texas prison system issued him a new convict number: #7712. Immediately after this development, on January 6, 1892, Hardin petitioned for a full pardon from the governor.

On November 6 his wife, Jane, passed away, leaving him with three grown children who had never really known him.

On January 1, 1893, he submitted another request for a pardon to Governor Hogg. This time he listed in detail the events of his conviction and the reasons he felt the sentence had been unjust. It was obvious his law studies were being converted into practice and he was pleading his own case to the governor. Citing from his law books in his prison cell, Wes Hardin made his case for his innocence, refusing—as he would until his death—to admit any responsibility for the murder he was charged with.

His petition and the hundreds of other letters and petitions from outside Huntsville finally paid off in 1894 when John Wesley Hardin walked out of the Huntsville prison unit on February 17. He had spent fifteen years, eight months, and twelve days behind prison bars.

In many ways John Wesley Hardin epitomized the justification for pardon or parole from prison. The first third of his time served had been defined by involvement in escape attempts, extended periods in solitary confinement, subjection to flogging and the other tortures of prison guards, and general rebellion against the prison officials and all authority. The final ten years of his sentence had been characterized by personal development: study of theology and law, teaching Sunday school, participating in a debating society, petitioning the legislature for penal reforms, and adherence to prison rules.

If ever an ex-convict walked out through the front doors of the Huntsville Walls Unit "appearing" to be a reformed man, John Wesley Hardin certainly fit the image.

He immediately applied for and was admitted to the Texas bar and moved back to Gonzales to practice. There, however, his reputation and past actions were a constant problem, so he moved to Junction and married a seventeen-year-old girl.

At Junction his marriage failed after a few weeks, and Hardin moved to Pecos to help in the trial of one of his relatives. After that he made possibly the biggest mistake of his life.

After the Pecos trial Hardin moved out west to El Paso—the most wide-open, lawless town in Texas. It was also the poorest possible choice for a home to a reforming gunslinger trying to practice law.

In El Paso, in 1895, he did try to become a legitimate attorney by setting up shop and passing out business cards. He also returned to many of his old habits: excessive drinking, gambling, and hanging around saloons and other disreputable places. He took as a client a horse thief named Martin Morose hiding out across the Rio Grande River. On the El Paso side of the river, however, Mrs. Morose moved in with Wes Hardin. Hardin's new live-in girlfriend was also a known prostitute in El Paso's wide-open red light district. The district may have been wide open, but the working girls were expected to pay "license fees" for protection. Mrs. Morose preferred to freelance, and it is generally conceded that Wes Hardin had become her "protector" from the established sporting houses and corrupt law officials.

One of those law officers was another notorious gunslinging outlaw named John Selman, who was constable of El Paso in 1895. While the position of constable would appear to indicate Selman was working on the side of the law, in reality he was using the position as an "enforcer" for the operators of the whorehouses, gambling halls, and saloons of El Paso. As such, Hardin's protection of his freelancing "live-in" would put both of them at odds with the sporting crowd of El Paso.

On the Mexican side of the Rio Grande, Mr. Morose was understandably upset at Hardin's relationship with his wife and swore revenge. One night Morose was crossing the rail bridge to El Paso (possibly to kill Hardin) when he was ambushed and killed. Reportedly a large amount of cash was removed from the body.

Many speculated it was John Wesley Hardin who did the killing himself that night, but other sources claimed Hardin had hired a gang of four law officers to do the murder. One of those officers, El Paso rumors held, was John Selman. Two other lawmen, Jeff Milton and George Scarborough (a U.S. deputy marshal), were allegedly involved. The fourth member of this assassination team, some have claimed, was none other than John Wesley Hardin himself.

Today, over a century later, rumors and conspiracy theories abound concerning the murder of Morose and the events that transpired afterwards. But one thing is certain: Morose was dead and a large wad of money was missing.

Selman and Hardin, who had bad blood between them over the issue of the dead man's wife hustling in El Paso without a license, no doubt viewed each other as enemies despite their alliance in the Morose killing (if, in fact, they were co-conspirators).

Among the rash of rumors flooding El Paso after the Morose killing was the allegation that Selman had been left out when the money taken from the body was split up. It's still conjecture, but if Hardin was responsible for commissioning the murder and he and Selman were on the outs, it's very likely Wes Hardin would have snubbed the constable simply out of spite.

At any rate, on August 19, 1895, John Selman approached Hardin from behind in the Acme Saloon and shot him twice in the back of the head. The legendary John Wesley Hardin was dead: ambushed from behind.

Selman was tried for the murder of Hardin, but because of a hung jury he was released on bond. On April 6, 1896, George Scarborough killed Selman in a shootout. Scarborough was acquitted of murder, but this final incident only fueled the conspiracy theories concerning the deaths of Morose and Hardin.

During his lifetime, John Wesley Hardin faced off and killed between forty and fifty men in what are generally considered to be fair fights. In fact, it was only through ambush from behind that any man bested him in a gunfight. Over the decades other outlaws and gunslingers would create Texas legends, but to this day John Wesley Hardin remains the baddest of the badmen.

His reputation was built quickly and at a young age. He died when he was only forty-two years old. Given the fact he had spent nearly sixteen years at Huntsville, he had spent half of his adult life behind Texas prison walls where he killed no man. But even in prison he remained a badman.

When he walked out through the main gate at Huntsville in 1894, his gunslinging days were behind him, but his prison experience only served to add to his mystique and legend. Gunfighter, killer, gambler, consort of prostitutes, Sunday school teacher, debate club president, lawyer—Texas has never seen the likes of Wes Hardin before or since his death in 1895.

And the Texas prison system has never had a prisoner like John Wesley Hardin before or since his imprisonment at Huntsville from 1878 to 1894.

1   Hardin, John Wesley, *The Life of John Wesley Hardin As Written by Himself* (Seguin, Texas: Smith and Moore, 1896).

2   Metz, Leon, *John Wesley Hardin, Dark Angel of Texas* (El Paso: Mangan Books, 1966).

3   Ibid., pg. 202.

Chapter Two

"Old Sparky"—The Texas Electric Chair

Stories, like pure rumors, take on a pulse of their own inside prison walls and often become absurd. There is an old, old saying in prison: "Don't believe anything you hear and only half of what you see!" It's good advice.

Convicts, often by necessity, exaggerate greatly most of what they tell other inmates. Sometimes it is to impress and intimidate; other times it is done to establish territory on the cell blocks; at times it is simply to help pass the monotony of slow-moving time on a seemingly motionless calendar.

But as a result, much of what one hears inside the walls and chain link fencing of a prison unit is suspect. That goes for not just stories about the inmates but about the prison itself. Then at some point it almost becomes impossible to tell truth from myth.

Such a case is the story of "Old Sparky."

Old Sparky is a piece of inmate-built furniture—an oak chair of rather plain but very durable construction. Even the official prison archives are unclear about some aspects of its history. But Old Sparky remains today the most famous piece of furniture ever produced by the legions of convict craftsmen over the past century and a half.

The reason is that Old Sparky served as the prison system's electric chair over four decades until 1964. Even the beginning date of the chair's service for the state is debated, but more about that in a moment.

It is believed that the first execution by electricity in the United States occurred on August 6, 1890, when William Kemmler was electrocuted in New York.

At that time Texas law stipulated that executions be conducted in the county in which the criminal was assessed the death penalty. A common feature in many Texas county courthouses or jails was the gallows chamber with the lynch beam and trap door. Many are still open to the public today as county museums. The individual responsible for administering the hangings was the county sheriff—and some over the years had become experts at their trade.

By 1923 at least twelve states had adopted electrocution as the officially sanctioned form of administering the death penalty. In Texas, alleged abuses by county juries and over-zealous sheriffs in conjunction with an alarming rise in illegal lynching led to a call for Texas to also adopt electrocution and centralize the administration of the executions at the prison headquarters in Huntsville.

Texas adopted the electric chair that year in the form of Senate Bill 160 of the Second Called Session of the Thirty-eighth Legislature. That bill authorized electrocution as a jury option for convictions of robbery, rape, and murder. The bill specified that such executions were to be conducted "after midnight and before sunrise"—a stipulation that was followed until Old Sparky was retired in 1964. Over the decades, the story circulated among prisoners and even in the media that inmates who were allowed to "see the light of day" on their assigned execution date were automatically granted a thirty-day stay of execution.

In fact that practice had been in effect for many years with regards to the hangman. Such was the case, but it was not due to the provisions of Senate Bill 160. More likely, that option continued with Old Sparky at the discretion of the warden of the Huntsville unit, and the practice was maintained as a prison rule rather than as the result of state law. No doubt most if not all of the condemned prisoners being led to the chair held out hope that something would malfunction long enough to grant them thirty more days of life. Occasionally their prayers would be answered. Sometimes, with the promise of coming rays of dawn, convicts would be brutally teased as malfunctions were hastily repaired—one inmate made a total of three trips to the chair before it successfully killed him.

But in 1923 such death row custom with regards to the electric chair had not been formalized. The first chair is believed to have been built by an inmate named Belton Harris, convicted of murder in Athens, Texas, in 1914 and spared through an execution stay by the governor's office. He reportedly had his sentence commuted and was eventually released. Harris, if he did in fact build the chair, constructed it of native Texas oak, and the new contraption was installed in the Huntsville death chamber on December 1, 1923.

Old Sparky can be viewed today at the Texas Prison Museum in Huntsville. During the 1990s the museum was located on the courthouse square in an old bank building—the chair itself located inside a vault and shielded by Plexiglas but very accessible for viewing by the public.

After the U.S. Supreme Court banned capital punishment in the United States as a violation of the Eighth Amendment "cruel and unusual" prohibition, Old Sparky was retired in 1964. At that time the chair was taken apart and moved to a wooden crate next to the execution chamber at the Walls Unit in Huntsville. In 1982, when Texas again began using capital punishment, lethal injection was approved as a more humane method of execution.

Old Sparky remained packed away in its crate until the Texas Prison Museum was created and the old chair reassembled as the focal point of the exhibits. And it was billed as the original "Texas Thunderbolt" or "Old Sparky."

But in 1987 a Colorado man claimed he had the first Texas electric chair—an old oak chair he had purchased from a New Mexico roadside freak show. And again, like so many other prison stories, it becomes almost impossible to ascertain truth from myth. His chair, he claimed, was the original Texas Thunderbolt, and he had some basis for his claims.

In Texas, archivists began digging into the history of Old Sparky, and it was discovered that newspaper reports and some very old memories recalled the original use of a wooden electric chair that did not always exactly match up with the Old Sparky in the Texas Prison Museum.

The researchers did find a relative of an early Texas executioner who recalled two different chairs and remembered being shown the new chair, called Old Sparky, when it was put inside the execution chamber in the 1930s. The original chair, the relative recalled, was loaned to a sheriff after 1930 for a convention or party and never returned.

If his memory was correct, and many prison authorities feel it was, then Texas did in fact have two electric chairs: the Texas Thunderbolt and Old Sparky.

The chair alleged to be the Texas Thunderbolt, if authentic, would be the piece constructed by Belton Harris. While similar in appearance, the Texas Thunderbolt is constructed of oak veneer and is actually a rather attractive piece of furniture. But it is much more flimsy than Old Sparky, and therein lies the basis for which many authorities are convinced it was the first electric chair in Texas.

From the first executions on February 8, 1924, a problem with this new form of death penalty was the fact that the condemned men jerked, twisted, and lurched as the current was applied through the electrodes. Witnesses in newspaper accounts document this. Those accounts, coupled with the recollections of a replacement chair, would explain why Old Sparky was used as a replacement in 1930.

Old Sparky is of far sturdier construction than the alleged Texas Thunderbolt and has more braces, solid oak construction, and a more efficiently designed heavy neck restraint. In other words, it provided a macabre version of the old saying, "Right tool for the right job."

But if the Colorado chair is the true Texas Thunderbolt—and not everyone believes it is—it would be Belton Harris' chair in which forty-eight criminals died between 1924 and 1930.

But officially, at least, Old Sparky remains the Texas electric chair in which a total of 361 men died between February 1924 and July 1964.

Senate Bill 160, in addition to replacing hanging with electrocution as the method of death penalty, also removed the responsibility for execution from the county sheriffs and transferred it to the warden of the Huntsville prison unit where the new Death House was established. After the installation of the chair on December 1, 1923, the first executions were scheduled for February 8, 1924, when five men were scheduled to die.

The warden at Huntsville, however, Captain R.F. Coleman, harbored strong feelings about his new assigned duty as "state executioner." On February 4, 1924, Captain Coleman resigned rather than assume the new legislated role of his office. The mission of a prison system was to rehabilitate, not kill, he claimed in a statement that bucked the conventional thinking of prison authorities in Texas and most of the United States during the 1920s.

But another warden was promoted, and on February 8, 1924, five men were executed—the first being Mack Matthews. Four decades later, on July 30, 1964, Joseph Johnson, a murderer from Harris County, was the last man to die in

Old Sparky. During those four decades a total of 361 men met their deaths seated and strapped in the chair.

Another myth that has persisted regarding the electric chair in Texas is that some women were also executed. Of the 506 criminals sentenced to death during Old Sparky's tenure, several of those convicted were women. But in the history of the electric chair in Texas, no woman was ever executed by Old Sparky or even the Texas Thunderbolt.

But 361 men were. And the stories, myths, and legends were born and exaggerated.

In 1994 a book titled *The Rope, the Chair, and the Needle: Capital Punishment in Texas, 1923-1990* chronicled many of the facts and folklore of Old Sparky's service to Texas. Among the facts reported were:

- *The youngest offender:* Henderson Young (#196), a convicted rapist executed in 1938 just days before his seventeenth birthday.

- *The oldest person executed:* Clemens Matura, executed at age 67 in 1937.

- *Five executions in one night:* the night of February 8, 1924.

- *Three executions in one night:* December 29, 1933, February 9, 1934, and July 10, 1936.

- *Two executions in one night:* twenty-two occurrences.

- *First execution in which a female reporter was allowed to witness:* the 1927 electrocution of E.M. Snow.

- *First inmate executed for killing another Texas convict:* Sam Phillips in 1926.

- *Brothers executed:* Frank and Lorenzo Noel in 1925, S.A. and Forest Robins in 1926, Oscar and Mack Brown in 1936, and Roscoe and Henderson Young in 1938.[1]

The mechanics of Old Sparky were relatively simple. A century after the 1890 electrocution in New York, several states—notably Florida—were still utilizing the same basic technology.

In Texas 1,800 volts of current were used to kill the condemned man. In the words of witnesses, the sound of the execution would begin with a crunching sound, followed by a hum that increased in intensity until it became a whine and then, finally, a "snarl."

The administration of the current, likewise, had changed very little since the inception of the electric chair. The condemned man would enter the chamber to be instructed by the warden, ironically, to "take a seat." Once seated, the inmate would have electrodes applied to his head and left leg. Several methods have been used to facilitate the transfer of current from the electrodes to the skin—contemporary use of wetted sponges has been controversial—but Texas used a saline solution. The electrodes applied, the convict's arms would be fastened to the armrests of Old Sparky with heavy leather straps. Likewise, the legs would be fastened tightly to the chair legs and the torso of the body strapped tautly against the back of the chair to reduce jerking and bucking against the current. Cotton would then be stuffed into the nostrils (to prevent the flow of blood from ruptured brain cells) just prior to a mask being placed over the head.

The warden would inspect the preparations, signal the executioner behind a one-way mirror, and the current would be applied.

"Crunch." "Whine." "Snarl."

Relegated to a museum piece today, Old Sparky was responsible for the execution of 361 inmates from 1924 to 1964. (photo by Gary Brown)

Death was usually achieved within a few minutes. But sometimes death did not come quickly—or easily. Many executed men fought frantically against the straps that held them, and smoke often was emitted from the areas of the leg and head from which the electrodes were attached. Often, condemned did not die quietly, but choked and gasped as the electric chair merely burned them, rather than killing them. The worst characteristic usually described after an execution was the sickening smell of burned flesh.

In 1925 a former sheriff named Clem Gray, convicted of murder, was executed after he had slashed his wrists and throat in a last-minute attempt at suicide. It was later recalled by several witnesses as the goriest execution ever by the electric chair. Old Sparky was efficient, but it was not kind.

Over the four decades of use, Old Sparky executed several convicts who had achieved a measure of infamy or notoriety for their crimes. Among two of the most publicized executions were the May 10, 1935 executions of Raymond Hamilton and Joe Palmer.

In the sensational and successful escape from Eastham orchestrated by Clyde Barrow and Bonnie Parker in 1934, Hamilton and Palmer had killed Major Crowson before being recaptured and sentenced to death for the murders.

At the time, prison director Lee Simmons had sworn vengeance for all involved in the escape and death of his officers. Former Texas Ranger Frank Hamer had taken care of Bonnie and Clyde. Old Sparky took care of Joe Palmer and Raymond Hamilton.

Today lethal injection has replaced Old Sparky just as the chair replaced the noose in 1924. Relegated to a position of curiosity in a museum setting, Old Sparky remains today one of the best-known aspects of Texas prison history. But to its very last act on July 30, 1964, Old Sparky was efficient but it was never kind.

1   Marquart, James W., *et al.*, *The Rope, the Chair, and the Needle: Capital Punishment in Texas 1923-1990* (Austin: University of Texas Press, 1994), pp. 33-34.

Chapter Three

"Shine Her Ever Lovin' Light on Me"—"Leadbelly"

Twenty miles southwest of downtown Houston lies a large plot of farmland at the intersection of State Highway 6 and Alternate Highway 90 near the community of Sugarland.

Located in one of the fastest growing areas in the Houston metropolitan area, the farm area is an anachronism and a relic of the past. Forming a boundary on one side, railroad tracks run alongside Highway 90—cutting across the only entrance to the farm and backing up traffic intermittently throughout the day and night. Located about a mile inside the tracks is the Central prison farm—formerly known as the Sugarland Unit.

In the late 1800s the land was developed for the production of sugar cane, and much of the labor had been provided through the convict lease system to the Imperial Sugar Company in Fort Bend County. In 1908 the state bought the Imperial Farm, a 5,235-acre land unit, from the company and named it the Sugarland Unit.

The prison was developed as a farm unit designated primarily for black inmates. Much of the land was used for cultivation of sugar cane, cotton, corn, feed crops, and vegetables. In 1931 the name was changed to the Central Unit. And throughout this development, the Southern Pacific trains continued to pass by the property, their whistles and lights seemingly taunting the work squads in the fields by day and teasing the convicts locked inside the bunker-like concrete buildings after dark.

One particular night train, a Southern Pacific, left Houston every night at shortly after eleven for San Antonio and West Texas. From Houston's Union Station, it passed through Fort Bend County about twenty miles west and into the Brazos River and Oyster Creek bottomlands where the Sugarland Unit was located. The train was called the Midnight Special, and to the inmates locked up inside the prison unit, the sounds of the whistles and beams of lights around midnight each night became a constant reminder of life beyond the prison fences.

This much was true; and from these facts has grown the legend of the famous blues singer Leadbelly and his composition of one of his greatest hits while he was assigned here as a Texas inmate titled, appropriately, "The Midnight Special."

Today the Central Unit, like all other Texas prison units, has undergone modernization and change. But in the midst of one of the fastest developing areas of Houston, the old concrete prison structures—painted white—and the squads of convicts working the fields in prison uniforms provide a stark reminder of the purpose of the property and how little some things change with the passage of time.

And still the trains continue to run along the railroad tracks night and day. Southern Pacific's Midnight Special is long gone, but it was along these tracks that one of Texas's most enduring convict stories was born. Unfortunately, most of the story is probably just that—an inmate story based upon some scraps of fact and a lot of exaggerated myth.

The problem is that America was literally crisscrossed with railroad tracks in the early 1920s, and in almost any community where a train passed regularly around midnight, that train was referred to as the Midnight Special. There were also, across America, Noon Specials, Supper Specials, and Wake-up Specials. And music about trains has always been—and still is today—popular. Something about the lonesome sound of a faraway train whistle has historically called to the musical composers of this country.

Almost certainly a song—or several songs—about Midnight Specials were circulating throughout the country when Huddie William Ledbetter was assigned to the Sugarland Unit in the late 1920s, serving time for murder. And most probably he didn't compose his famous rendition from scratch while serving time there. Rather, he likely took a song being bandied about by the work squads in the sugar cane fields and rearranged it. Such practices were common during these years. Most music historians doubt that he actually authored the song, but no one doubts that his arrangement became the standard recognized literally around the world today.

Ledbetter was born sometime between 1885 and 1888 on a plantation near Mooringsport, Louisiana. He was the only child of Wesley Ledbetter, a tenant farmer, and Sally Pugho. The family moved from Louisiana to East Texas when he was very young, and it is thought that it was in Texas that his musical interests were developed with the help of an uncle who gave him an accordion.

From the accordion, however, he quickly moved to the six-string guitar, and he is reported to have left home in 1901 to wander around as a minstrel. He would have been between the ages of twelve and fifteen if this is true, but such ventures were not unheard of at the end of the nineteenth century.

If this experience helped broaden his musical education, it undoubtedly also broadened his overall education—and in ways that assured Huddie Ledbetter would be at odds with the law almost all of his life.

Working, while still a child, in the whorehouses and saloons along Fannin Street in Shreveport, he continued to develop his guitar and singing skills while doing odd jobs—whatever odd tasks a young boy could hustle in the bordellos, gambling parlors, and beer halls of Shreveport. It was by no means a traditional or classical education—by musical or lifestyle standards.

Later, as he grew physically and musically, he moved back to Texas and worked the rougher areas of Dallas and Fort Worth. He spent summers working as a farmhand and continued singing and playing his guitar in saloons and dance halls during the winter.

By the age of twenty-one he had become a full-time wandering musician and, in the process, had assumed drinking and gambling habits from the violent bars and saloons he performed in.

It was in Dallas that he met another blues singer named Blind Lemon Jefferson, and the two quickly became partners with Jefferson as the mentor and Ledbetter the student—the latter converting finally to the twelve string guitar.

But while he was developing musically, the lifestyle was taking its toll on him. In 1916 he was in a Texas jail on charges of assaulting a woman. Assigned to a chain gang, he somehow managed to escape and spent the next two years under the alias of Walter Boyd. But the pattern had already been established, and brushes with the law would become a fact of his life in the coming years.

A year later, in 1917, he was involved in another fight, supposedly over a woman, and this time he killed a man and was convicted of murder and sentenced to a thirty-year term of hard labor at the Huntsville state prison. From Huntsville he was transferred to the Shaw State Prison Farm on the Red River in Bowie County.

Again he tried to escape, but prison was tougher than county jail, and the failed attempt resulted in another six years being added to his sentence. He was eventually transferred to the Sugarland Unit southwest of Houston where he was assigned to work in the sugar cane fields. It was here that he later recalled listening to and participating in the inmate ritual of singing in the fields and communicating with each other in sing-song phrases laced with musical expressions. It was a form of communication in which the men shouted back and forth, trading lines of a song or creating new words to a familiar tune.

It likely was the basis for which, resting in his bunk at nights, listening to the whistle of the Midnight Special, and perhaps watching its light beam in the darkness through the bars of his cell, he rearranged the words to his rendition of that song in his head.

It is also thought that it was during his stay at the Sugarland Unit that he picked up the nickname "Leadbelly." Exactly why he assumed this particular nickname is impossible to prove. It may have simply been a play on his given name of "Ledbetter," but other rumors attribute it to his having received a gunshot to the stomach, his breakneck pace working the chain gangs, or even his proclaimed sexual prowess. But the legend of Leadbelly was created at Sugarland in the early 1920s.

Prison officials there allowed him to continue playing the guitar in the evenings, and Leadbelly later recalled that his years at Sugarland were also a period of productive song writing and arranging.

Another of the legends attributed to him while he was in prison there had to do with one of those songs he had written. This story does appear to be true.

In the seventh year of Leadbelly's sentence, in 1925, Governor Pat Neff visited the Sugarland prison unit during the final days of his administration. Governor Neff had served two terms as Texas governor and during that period had achieved the reputation of opposing executive pardons or clemency for inmates of the prison system. As a matter of record, he left office in 1925 having signed only ninety-two pardons in four years.

Leadbelly must have been aware of this when the governor visited Sugarland. Somehow, he got prison officials to agree to his approaching the governor and dedicating a song to him. No known prison records indicate the exact circumstances of the serenade—if the governor was seated and Leadbelly standing or sitting—but he was allowed to sing the following words to Governor Pat Neff:

> *Please, Governor Neff, Be good 'n' kind*
> *Have mercy on my great long time . . .*
> *I don't see to save my soul*
> *If I don't get a pardon, try me on a parole . . .*
> *If I had you, Governor Neff, like you got me*
> *I'd wake up in the mornin' and I'd set you free*

Surprisingly, the usually pardon-stingy Governor Neff was convinced by the song and by Leadbelly's assurances that he'd seen the error of his ways. In one of his final acts as governor, Neff pardoned Leadbelly and released him from prison. The legend of Leadbelly continued to grow.

A major part of the Leadbelly legend in later years was that he had twice sung his way to executive clemency—once in Texas and once in Louisiana. The Texas pardon is documented fact, but the Louisiana pardon appears to be mythical.

After his release from the Texas prison system, Leadbelly migrated back over to Louisiana and quickly got into trouble. By 1930 he was arrested, tried, and convicted of attempted homicide and sentenced to "hard time" in Louisiana's notorious Angola prison unit.

While serving time there, he was "discovered" by Texas folklorist John Avery Lomax and his son Alan. The Lomaxes recorded Leadbelly while he was at Angola and campaigned for a pardon or his early release. One of those recordings would become his most popular composition and was attributed to his receiving a pardon from the Louisiana governor's office. Louisiana officials deny this, and this story, at least, appears to be only one of the many myths surrounding the story of Leadbelly.

Ironically, it was while Leadbelly was at Angola in Louisiana, on July 16, 1933, that he recorded the song that most identified him with the Texas prison system and created the story of the "Midnight Special."

Midnight Special

Words and music by Huddie Ledbetter
Collected and adapted by John A. Lomax and Alan Lomax

One day, one day, Sir
I was walking along
I heard that special
Singing a lonesome song

Chorus:
Oh, let the Midnight Special
Shine her light on me
Let the Midnight Special
Shine her ever lovin' light on me

If you ever go to Houston
You know you better walk right
You know you better not stagger
You know you better not fight
Because the sheriff will just arrest you
You know he'll carry you down
And you can bet your bottom dollar
Oh Lord, you're penitentiary bound

Chorus

Yonder come little Rosie
How in the world do you know?
I can tell her by her apron
And the dress she wore
Umbrella on her shoulder
Piece of paper in her hand
Goes a marchin' to the Captain
Says I want my man

Chorus

Now here comes jumpin' Judy
I'll tell you how I know
You know, Judy brought jumpin'
To the whole wide world
She brought it in the morning
Just about the break of day
You know, if I ever get to jumpin'
Oh Lord, I'll up and jump away.

©1936, 1959, 1964 (renewed) TRO-Folkways Music Publishers, Inc. (BMI)

There can be little doubt that prison life in Texas affected Leadbelly's arrangement of the song—references to "singing a lonesome song" and "shine her ever lovin' light on me" differ dramatically from other traditional arrangements of the same song.

A much later rendition of the song by Credence Clearwater Revival, listing the credit as "traditional—arranged by John Fogerty," opened the song with the words:

> Well, you wake up in the mornin',
> you hear the work bell ring,
> And they march you to the table
> to see the same old thing.
> Ain't no food upon the table,
> and no pork up in the pan.
> But you better not complain, boy,
> you get in trouble with the man.

The Swedish rock group ABBA also recorded a version of "Midnight Special" in which the opening was yet another variation of the Credence "traditional" arrangement:

> Well, you wake up in the morning
> Hear the ding dong ring
> You go marching to the table
> See the same old thing
> See the food on the table
> Nothing in your pan
> If you say anything about it
> You're in trouble with the man

Both groups and many other recorders of "Midnight Special" credit Leadbelly for inspiring their recording of the song, but the fact remains that he probably did not write it. He did, however, arrange the most popular version and certainly was responsible for the song being recognized worldwide by generations of music lovers after his Angola recording.

After his release from Louisiana—prison officials there still insist his release was based upon "good-time" credits and not executive clemency—he toured with the Lomaxes, giving concerts and recording the massive amount of arrangements he had developed over the years in Texas and Louisiana prisons.

As he began to develop a national prominence, he was convicted of assault again in 1939 and imprisoned at New York's Riker Island prison unit.

He died in New York City on December 6, 1949, of amyotrophic lateral sclerosis, commonly known as Lou Gehrig's disease. He was buried at Shiloh Baptist Church, north of Shreveport, Louisiana.

Much of his adult life (and his most productive musical years) was spent behind prison walls. But in the periods of freedom between sentences, he impacted his genre of music tremendously. At various times, his associates included Woody Guthrie, Pete Seger, and Sonny Terry.

Later, individuals with backgrounds as diverse as Johnny Cash, Kurt Cobain, and John Fogerty would record versions of his works. Leadbelly's most popular composition, "Goodnight Irene," achieved its greatest success in the early 1950s after his death, when the Weavers recorded it.

In 1980 the Nashville Songwriters Association inducted him into their International Hall of Fame. That honor was followed in 1986 with membership in the Blues Foundation Hall of Fame, and in 1988 his work was honored by the Rock and Roll Hall of Fame. In 1988 Louisiana erected a historical marker at his gravesite.

Back in Texas, a huge mural of him is prominently displayed near the downtown courthouse square in Huntsville, but otherwise the prison system does not promote his musical accomplishments while incarcerated. His presence seems to be slowly fading away.

Unless, of course, you count the occasional train that passes the Central Unit (formerly the Sugarland Unit)—

This mural on a downtown Huntsville building is one of the very few memorials in Texas to an inmate who immortalized a Texas train from his cell at the old Sugarland Unit. (photo by Gary Brown)

sometimes around midnight—"singing a lonesome song" and "shining her ever lovin' light . . . "

Today inmates and guards alike at Central are likely to point across the fields to the railroad tracks and tell you for fact that "Ole Leadbelly sat in a cell here and wrote 'Midnight Special.'"

As is usual with Texas prison stories, fact is interspersed with myth. And part of their claim is true. Anyway it makes for a good story.

And, seventy-five years after his presence at Sugarland, the train whistles still "sing a lonesome song" and head beams "shine their ever lovin' lights."

Some things are true and never change.

The Early Texas prison system operated on strictly segregated units such as this unnamed farm unit during the 1950s. (photo source: Texas State Archives, courtesy of Jester III Unit, Texas Department of Criminal Justice).

Chapter Four

"The Scab Building"?—Texas State Capitol

From the earliest days of the Republic of Texas until statehood and even today, Texas has never hesitated to attempt what others considered the impossible or controversial. Sitting at the head of Congress Avenue in Austin, the Texas state capitol represents one of those "impossible" stories. And while some would say that in Texas nothing is impossible, it may also be true that nothing in Texas is without controversy.

Today the Texas Capitol is the largest of all state capitol buildings and second in total size only to the National Capitol in Washington, D.C. But size is not the only notable story behind its construction. Although completed in 1888, it was conceived in post-Civil War Reconstruction when Texas was rich in undeveloped land but bankrupt in hard currency.

Lack of cash was not a problem, according to Texan politicians who drafted Section 57 of Article VI of the Texas Constitution of 1876, providing for the sale of 3,000,000 acres of land in the Panhandle area in exchange for a permanent capitol building. It was a concept never attempted before: exchanging public lands for construction of a permanent capitol building.

When there was no money to pay the surveying teams, the politicians merely tacked on another 50,000 acres to pay the surveyors.

After a controversy over the exterior stone, a free source of Texas pink granite was obtained near Burnet and Marble Falls. Then another problem developed during construction: There was no money available to hire skilled quarrymen to cut and remove the pink granite.

The solution again was simple—use convicts from the prison system. And thus the controversy.

But the use of convict labor was a concept that did not develop until well into the overall plans for the capitol building.

While the Constitution of 1876 set aside three million acres of Panhandle land to fund construction, it was not until 1879 that a capitol board was established and plans initiated for the surveying of ten counties in far North Texas.

By late 1880 the surveying was completed and a competition was announced for architectural plans. In May of 1881 the plans submitted by a Detroit firm were approved. The capitol board then advertised for a contractor who would build the state capitol building in exchange for the three million acres of land in the Panhandle. An Illinois bid was accepted and subcontracted to a Chicago firm in 1882.

By this time controversy was well embedded in the process. Some opposed the dispensation of public land; others disliked the final architectural plans; and still others opposed awarding the construction contract to an out-of-state builder. But overall the process was moving along, and it looked like Texas was going to actually pull off the first ever land-for-a-state-capitol trade.

Then the really big controversy hit Austin.

The original legislative directive specified that construction of the exterior of the building should be of native limestone, and a railroad had been built from the Oatmanville quarry nine miles west of Austin to the capitol site at the head of Congress Avenue. It was completed in March of 1884. Ten derricks were placed at the railhead—each with a sixty-five-foot mast and a fifty-foot boom that could handle up to ten tons of material. Two elevated railways handled the heavy building stone.

But the initial delivery of Oatmanville limestone varied in color and was subject to discoloring stains because of iron particles in the rock. The owners of Granite Mountain quarries near Marble Falls in Burnet County offered the state free pink granite, and the problem appeared to be solved.

The contractor, however, refused to work with granite since it would be more difficult and therefore more expensive to build with. Again, a compromise was reached: Texas would modify the original architectural plans, and the state would take care of any "extra cost" by constructing a narrow-gauge railroad from Burnet to Granite Mountain and furnish up to five hundred convict laborers to quarry the stone. The contractor would pay the state for the use of the convicts and provide room and board for them.

And so "breaking rocks in the hot sun" became a reality initially for 300 prisoners who were to earn for the state 65 cents per day per convict. Only, these rocks were "Texas-sized" boulders of almost metallic density.

The work would be backbreaking and dangerous, and trained union quarrymen at that time earned around $4 per day. The convict-lease idea at 65 cents per day seemed an excellent choice at the time.

The state prisoners completed the fifteen-mile narrow gauge railroad from the granite quarry to Marble Falls in November of 1885, and room and board facilities for the convicts were established at the quarry.

Despite protests by union and labor organizations that eventually
became an international incident, these Texas inmates rough-cut and
excavated the granite stone for the Texas capitol building.

The use of free—or almost free—convict labor in the quarries, however, was seen as an attempt by the state to
undermine free labor and was opposed by virtually every
organized labor group in Austin. To further antagonize the
union quarrymen, the contractor attempted to advertise for
additional "free world" nonunion workers to come to Austin to
assist.

Things were looking ugly in Austin at this point. While
untrained state prisoners could be used in manual tasks at
quarrying the raw stone at Marble Falls, they were incapable
of doing the finishing work or the actual stonework on the
exterior of the capitol building.

In September 1885 the Granite Cutter's International
Union posted the following question to its members:

A convict work crew works on one of the columns for the Texas state capitol building. Flat masonry is loaded on the rail cars to the right.

Having received information from our Graniteville secretary that it is contemplated by the syndicate who have the granite work, and have the contract for the Capitol Building to put on 200 granite cutters and 100 convicts about November 15, we consider that there is a vital principle involved in the matter, so we lay it before the union for instructions. If 200 granite cutters work with, and teach 100 convicts the trade the probability is that in twelve months time there would be but 100 granite cutters and the number of convicts would be increased to 200, and in two years time there would be 300 convicts and no free granite cutters whatever employed on the job, for if free granite cutters learn [sic] the convicts the trade, after the first lot is taught they will be put to teach other convicts, and thus drive out free labor altogether, for we have been reliably informed that the state officials of Texas have agreed to supply the contractors with 500 convicts. The National Union Committee therefore ask the Union what shall be done in the matter.

Question—Shall the National Union Committee issue an order in the name of the Union to granite cutters against working with convicts on the Texas State Capitol at Austin?[1]

The local union in Austin responded by calling a complete and total boycott of the capitol project and warned all non-union workers to stay out of Austin. In December 1885 the Union published the following notice in Austin:

Granite Cutters, keep away from Austin, Texas, until the contractors stop hiring convicts on the Austin state capitol building.

The sub-contractor said he would hire convicts, scabs and imported contract labor. Granite Cutters of America, show this Great-I-Am Gus Wilke [the contractor], and his employers...that free men will not submit to the introduction of slavery into our trade under the guise of contract convict labor, and that you will not teach convicts our trade to enrich these schemers, who care for nothing but the almighty dollar and now seek to degrade our trade to fill their own pockets.

The Austin State Capitol having been declared a scab job by the Granite Cutter's National Union, granite cutters are cautioned against cutting granite for it before the difficulty is settled satisfactorily.

Boycott the Austin, Texas, Capitol Building.[2]

In response, the Chicago-based contractor decided to break the boycott by importing eighty-six skilled workers from Scotland. The stonecutters arrived at New York only to be met by American union members and a U.S. marshal. Their recruitment, it turned out, was a violation of the Contract Labor Act of 1885.

From the prison walls of Huntsville, Texas, to Hadrian's Wall in Scotland, the use of Texas state prison convicts had created national and international repercussions.

Meanwhile at the Granite Mountain quarry, the prisoners continued to blast and cut the raw blocks of granite and load them for rail car shipment to Marble Falls and Austin.

To mark the first anniversary of the granite contract, a "public relations" trip was planned for members of the capitol board and the Texas prison administration. According to the *Austin Statesman*:

> A splendid dinner was served. There are at present 200 convicts engaged in quarrying and 100 in cutting the stone. There are also 148 regularly paid stone-cutters, making 448 men now at work dressing the granite for use here in Austin. The convicts are behaving well. The stone-cutters are perfectly satisfied. The quarries seem to be alive with men. Huge stones are piled up in every direction.[3]

In New York, union representatives persuaded twenty-four of the Scots to join the boycott, but sixty-four continued on to Texas. Their arrival in the capital led to a federal lawsuit against the Chicago-based company. Since their actions were obviously a violation of the Contract Labor Act of 1885, indictment was just a matter of time; however, postponements drug on until the summer of 1887. Meanwhile, the convicts continued working at Granite Mountain, and the nonunion Scottish stonecutters kept working in Austin.

Security measures were tight during the convict lease program at Burnet when Texas inmates were used to quarry granite for the state capitol building.

Mounted guards and dog trackers watch over the convicts leased out to quarry granite for the state capitol building. This undated photo was taken near the Marble Falls quarry.

The contractor eventually admitted the charges and was fined a total of $64,000, which was later reduced to $8,000 in 1893.

As part of the settlement, the number of convict workers was to be reduced, but records during that period indicate their numbers actually rose to 350 inmates. By the time of the 1887 indictment, however, most of the Scottish workers had departed Texas and there were only fifteen working on the capitol building in May of that year.

As unethical and illegal as it may have been, the use of convict and nonunion labor successfully broke the boycott and constructed the state capitol building. But from the quarry holes of Granite Mountain, Texas, to the ship docks of New York City to the workers' pubs of Aberdeen, Scotland, Texas prison inmates managed to stir up an enormous controversy, even by Texas standards.

Final work began on the dome in 1887, and the *Goddess of Liberty* was placed on top in February 1888. The capitol was opened to the public on April 21, 1888, and dedicated during May 14-19 of that year.

It proved to be a successful venture for all involved, except the Granite Cutters' International Union and the convicts who worked the quarries for no personal wages. Texas received a beautiful pink granite capitol building, and the contracting firm received three million acres of land in the Panhandle.

The land, in the ten counties of Deaf Smith, Parmer, Castro, Lamb, Bailey, Hockley, Dallam, Hartley, Cochran, and Oldham, was developed by a British investment firm into the XIT Ranch (Ten In Texas). In all, some 1,500 miles of land was fenced with barbed wire to contain up to 150,000 head of cattle. By 1913 the cattle had all been sold, and by 1929 most of the land had also been sold to individuals.

The total cost of the capitol was $3,744,630.60 with Texas paying only about $500,000. In 1888 the lands in the

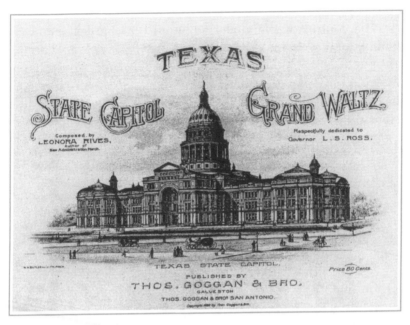

Panhandle wouldn't sell at 50 cents per acre; in 1998 those same lands had a tax evaluation of nearly $7 billion.

The Granite Cutters' International Union merged and became part of the Journeyman Stonecutters Association of North America in the 1960s and so far as is known has never removed the designation of "scab building" from the Texas capitol.

But today even the most hardened union worker would probably have to marvel at the beautiful century-old pink granite building at the head of Congress Avenue in Austin. Quite possibly the most beautiful public building in America and certainly of world-class architectural quality, it should be a source of pride to everyone connected with it.

Final construction of the building required an estimated 4,000 railroad cars of granite and 11,000 railroad cars of limestone and other materials. Much of that material was furnished through the cheap labor of Texas prison inmates who would never see the building themselves.

But if they could have, probably even they would have marveled at what they had helped create. And a few might have even chuckled at the national and international repercussions they had created in doing it.

The beautiful pink stone exterior of the Texas state capitol was quarried by the inmates under the convict lease program. (photo by Gary Brown)

Much controversy surrounded the construction of the Texas state capitol in the late 1800s. The use of inmate prisoners was one of the most criticized issues. (photo by Gary Brown)

1   Cotner, Robert C., *The Texas State Capitol* (Austin: The Pemberton Press, 1968), pg. 33.
2   Ibid., pg. 34 quoting the *Austin Statesman*, December 10, 1885.
3   *Austin Statesman*, January 31, 1886.

Chapter Five

"I've Always Wanted a Brick House"— Candy Barr

On December 4, 1959, yet another inmate was processed into the Texas prison system. Her name was Juanita Dale Phillips and she was "in her twenties." She arrived wearing a conservative black outfit and carrying nothing with her but a copy of the Bible. Immediately upon being processed, she was assigned Texas Department of Corrections Inmate Number 153781.

The conservative dress and the Bible, however, could not cover up the reputation of this inmate as one of Texas's most notorious—and sassy—striptease dancers. While being processed, she purportedly told prison authorities "I've always wanted a brick house."

Inmate #153781 was better known to Texas and the world as Candy Barr. And the image most Texans would have had of her that day was one in which she was in her skimpy cowboy outfit and pointing a toy pistol under a cocked leg. Her "cowboy outfit" consisted of boots, hat, a double holster, and little else.

With what has been called a "baby face" and a drop-dead gorgeous, heart-stopping five foot three, 36D ("Don't forget the D, mister")-23-36 figure, she undoubtedly was—and continues to be—probably the most beautiful and shapely inmate to ever do time in the Texas prison system.

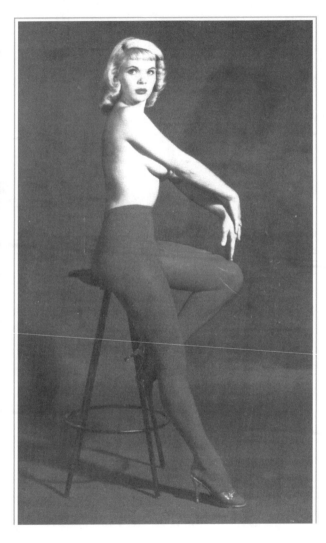

This late-1950s El Rancho Vegas Casino postcard from Las Vegas featuring Candy Barr was probably issued during the period of her appeal of her drug possession conviction. Her appeals failed, and she entered the Texas Department of Corrections in 1959.

Candy Barr was born Juanita Dale Slusher between 1933 and 1935 in Edna, Texas. Official records list her birth date as July 6, 1933, but she was always "elusive" when questioned about it.

Her childhood was difficult and troubled, and in 1951, while still a teenager, she performed in a short, fifteen-minute stag film titled *Smart Aleck*. Copies of the 8mm film are still around today and are considered collector's items in the adult film genre. *Smart Aleck* brought her instant fame for several reasons—in large part because of her beautiful face and shapely body—but it was also one of the very first non-simulated porno films ever produced for mass circulation.

But while *Smart Aleck* brought her fame, or at least notoriety, it was also indicative of her desire to "thumb her nose at society." It was said of her in later years that "trouble seemed to follow her around."

Trouble continued for Juanita Dale almost like falling dominoes after the release of *Smart Aleck*. In 1953 she married her second husband, and on January 27, 1956, she shot him with a .22 rifle. Because he survived and never pressed charges, she was not arrested that time.

By this period of her life she was becoming a well-known personality in Dallas under the stage name of Candy Barr. In the conservative, puritan Dallas of the 1950s, she danced at Southern Methodist University fraternity parties, posed for men's magazines, and began striptease dancing. Real trouble started when Candy became the headliner at Abe Weinstein's Colony Club, in the heart of Dallas' business district. Almost instantly she became the top drawing card, and Weinstein was hiring extra security to turn away the nightly overflow crowds. Anybody who was anybody in Dallas went to see Candy Barr dance—company presidents, lawyers, the district attorney, the mayor—virtually the Who's Who of Dallas at that time.

She headlined at the Colony Club but also developed a national reputation when she danced at New Orleans, Las Vegas, and Los Angeles. For a small-town Texas girl, she was making waves in the bright lights and tall buildings, and a lot of people didn't like it.

But the Colony Club remained her home base, and the moralists in Dallas could just take so much of Candy's thumbing of her nose and shaking of her fanny. And too, her activities at the club had put her in a position to see and hear a lot involving a considerable number of influential people in influential places. She was becoming a potential problem to some people besides the Morals Police in Dallas.

In 1957 she was busted on drug charges. At that time, and even today, suspicion existed that it was a setup—something Candy Barr has always insisted.

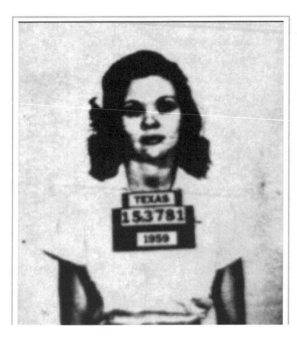

Candy Barr was processed into the Texas Department of Corrections on December 4, 1959, under the name Juanita Dale Phillips for drug possession charges that many, including Phillips, claimed were a police setup. She reportedly told reporters, "I've been old since I was 14."

Another dancer asked her to hold a small vial of marijuana seeds and stems, and she was immediately arrested and searched. The small bottle was found in her brassiere. If that wasn't enough, a marijuana cigarette was found "under her chair." All told, it was less than an ounce.

She was booked in Dallas County Jail in the fall of 1957 under the name of Juanita Dale Dabbs Phillips. The Morals Police succeeded temporarily in getting her off the stage at the Colony Club, but they never succeeded in breaking her rebellious spirit. "Make it sexy, boys," she reportedly told the police photographers when she was arrested.

While out on appeal, she continued removing her clothes at the Colony Club—drawing even larger crowds than before —and was reported to have earned up to $2,000 a week. She later said the money may have been there, but it never made it to her.

For two years she fought the drug bust charges, and her appeals eventually went all the way to the Supreme Court. It was during that appeals period that she met and became the companion of mob boss Mickey Cohen. Cohen reportedly hired San Francisco attorney Melvin Belli as her defense attorney.

Sometime around this period she also connected with Jack Ruby, although their relationship has never really been documented. She claims she had known him since she had been a very young teenager. Some reports claim Ruby acted as her manager and that she occasionally danced after hours at his Carrousel Club. Other reports, including Candy Barr herself, dispute those claims.

She went to court in 1958 for a four-day trial her lawyers called a "Roman carnival." The judge jumped from the bench at one point to take pictures of her himself. Despite strong indications the evidence was planted, she received a fifteen-year sentence in prison from a twelve-man jury for possession of less than an ounce of marijuana. The prosecution had wanted to go for life.

"I didn't even know how to fight the case. I don't think my lawyers had any grounds to work on. They were defeated before they began," she later claimed. When the verdict was announced, she gripped with her hands until her knuckles were white, bowed her head, and thanked the judge.[1]

Then she appealed.

She was in Las Vegas when she learned her bond had been forfeited and that a warrant had been issued on the grounds she was a fugitive from justice. Somehow it seems difficult to visualize one of America's most famous dancers headlining on a Las Vegas stage as a "fugitive," but agents of the FBI arrested her and escorted her back to Texas. It was, after all, the 1950s.

She had become a Texas legend while still in her twenties. From the small farm town of Edna she had traveled as far as the stages of places like New Orleans, Las Vegas, and Los Angeles.

That all came to a crashing end on December 4, 1959.

She reported to the Goree Unit of the Texas Department of Corrections, and while she may have wisecracked about always wanting a brick house, she also told reporters in a more somber note, "I've been old since I was fourteen." She was processed into the prison system and given a job assignment in the sewing room.

For a while she disappeared within those brick walls, and prison records indicate she was pretty much a model prisoner. In 1976 she told *Oui Magazine* "There was a point system in the penitentiary where I served my time. I really humped my buns to get 80 points. I worked in the sewing room, the library, and the commissary, and I performed in the prison rodeo. I even sang in both the Protestant and Catholic choirs."[2]

The program she was referring to was the newly instituted "Point Incentive Program" in which inmates were periodically rated by authorities with regards to participation in programs, job performance, attitude, and a complex scale of other factors. Once an inmate was eligible for parole, a score of 80 or better was required before the board would consider action.

If her activities behind the brick walls were all designed to accumulate Point Incentive Program or PIP points towards an early release, it was the Texas Prison Rodeo that simultaneously earned her points and kept her name, face, and famous body in front of the Texas public.

On October 2, 1960, she appeared at the 29th Annual Texas Prison Rodeo in Huntsville as a member of the Goree Girls band. She also did a solo version of Peggy Lee's song "Fever." The effect was electrifying. The "free-world" audience erupted in thunderous applause, and one can only imagine the reaction of the inmate population that day.

After singing, she told reporters that she was not nervous but that she intended to leave the entertainment business for good once she got out of prison. According to the *Houston Post*, she stated, "I'm going to become a housewife and a mother." Then she said, "However, as long as I am in prison, I will do whatever I can to help any program of rehabilitation."[3] The rebellious spirit was learning to "play the game."

The next week, October 9, 1960, she shared the billing with Sally Rand whom she had known at Las Vegas. She repeated her rendition of "Fever" while adding a few "stage gestures." The whistling from both the inmate and "free world" seats and the applause was reported to have "rocked the huge prison stadium." Those "stage gestures," however, were done without disrobing.

The third week of that rodeo season, Bo Diddley was the featured performer, but Candy Barr and the Goree Girls also thrilled the crowd. This time she changed her pace by singing a song she had written titled "Love, Honor, and Obey Blues."

The final week of the rodeo in 1960, October 23, the *Houston Post* reported the Goree Girls and Candy Barr matched Frankie Avalon in crowd appreciation, especially when Candy sang another composition she had written before entering prison named "Little Boy."

She was convicted and doing time in prison, but Candy Barr was back in the public's eye. After the 1960 rodeo season, she indicated that she didn't want to perform any more, and as the 1961 preparations were being made, the Goree Girls practiced their numbers without Candy.

By the first show of the 1961 season, however, she agreed at the last minute to sing with the Goree Girls again. She had, after all, "stolen" most of the 1960 shows, and one cannot help but wonder if TDC officials, following Abe Weinstein's example, didn't see a wealth of gate receipts in her appearances.

Nevertheless, on October 1, 1961, she did sing and stated that if she could help the other inmates, that was the thing she wanted to do. She was rewarded with a hearty applause.

A week later Rex Allen was the featured entertainer, and the *Post* reported that "although the crowds liked Allen, they also applauded . . . Candy Barr as she sang and danced with the Goree Girls."

She continued to match or outperform the "big name" rodeo attractions. On October 15 the *Post* announced, "Although Ernest Tubb drew a great deal of applause for his 'Grand Old Opry' tunes, Candy Barr received equal praise for her rendition of 'Fever.'"

The final week of the 1961 rodeo season she again performed her rendition of "Little Boy." She had completed her second annual rodeo and twenty-two months of her fifteen-year sentence.

Then, sometime during 1962, she got into a "scrape" with another inmate. It's not known with whom or over what issue, but as a result she was denied parole because of it that year. As she recalled in the *Oui* interview, "I wasn't a total goody-goody. I had to make a living, so I bootlegged toilet paper, delivered a few gifts, and operated a little illegal mail service."

On October 7, 1962, she was back on the stage at the Huntsville rodeo arena. The *Post* reviewed her performance reporting that "Wearing a black Western-style skirt and blouse much like the costumes for her former Dallas nightclub performances, she drew whistles of approval for her rendition of 'Bring It To Me.' With her hair drawn back in a long ponytail for the show, she appeared in the Goree Girl chorus and in two solo numbers."

The *Houston Post* reporter, no doubt, was later reminded that for her former Dallas nightclub performances, she wore much less than that. She may have been a "top draw" at the annual rodeo, but prison officials were not about to run that risk.

On October 21, 1962, she again performed with the Goree Girls, but her biggest applause came when the master of ceremonies, Lee Norton of Houston, announced that Candy Barr "hopes this year's rodeo will be the last one she will have to sing for as an inmate performer." It would appear the "scrape" and parole denial had been a lesson she had taken to heart.

In her final performance ever at the rodeo, October 28, 1962, it was reported she drew a big ovation following her rendition of a blues number.

Her career as a prison entertainer was over. Despite her status as an inmate, however, she had outperformed most of the Hollywood and Nashville stars headlining the prison rodeo programs, and the public had loved her. And it must have been rewarding to her to know the public had accepted her in a role other than disrobing on stage.

She came up for parole review again, and this time the Pardons Board, Texas Governor John Connally, and her trial court in Dallas had supported her parole application. She was paroled from the Texas prison system on April 1, 1963.

Prison officials honored her request to leave the Goree Unit unannounced and without media present. She was paid $5 in parole money and $5.70 for bus fare to her former home in Edna. Her discharge clothing had been sent to her—basically the same outfit she had reported to prison in nearly three and a half years earlier. It consisted of a black leather jacket, a black scarf, black skirt, and black high-heeled patent leather shoes; prison secretaries later characterized her dress that day as "chic."

She left the Goree Unit only to find there was nobody waiting to meet her. After returning to the unit she remained until Abe Weinstein (still owner of the Colony Club) and his wife picked her up to drive her to Edna.

While at Goree she had completed her high school diploma, become a trusty, and sung in the chapel choir as well as performing with the Goree Girls at the annual prison rodeos in 1960, 1961, and 1962. While inside, she had also written a book of poetry titled *A Gentle Mind . . . Confused*. It seemed an accurate personal assessment at the time.

Although she had requested anonymity in her release from prison, she spoke freely with United Press International over the telephone from Edna. "I do not intend to become a stripper again," she announced.[4] Texas parole law at that time prohibited her from returning to the night club circuit as a stripper or to frequent places that served alcoholic drinks.

"I plan to have some type of career and would like to go to orphanages and convalescent homes and help people. Everyone has been so kind to me," she continued.

Of her time in prison, she told the UPI, "I was happy to leave, of course. But I had been there quite some time and made a lot of friends. I'm going to miss them. I'm happy to be home."

Surprisingly free of bitterness, she confessed that her time in prison had given her a better outlook on life. "It gave me a better understanding of people. It made me stop and realize what I was missing out of life. The only regret I have is that it took me from my family."

The plans for a career in social work did not develop, however, and by her own admission she was not always in full compliance with her parole stipulations. After her parole she returned to Edna, and eight months after she was released she was struggling to make it financially when her old friend Jack Ruby came down for a three-day visit. Seven days later President Kennedy was assassinated, and Jack Ruby was thrust into the national limelight by shooting the accused killer on national TV.

Back in Edna, Candy Barr received another visit from the FBI. It was the 1960s after all.

In the whirlwind of conspiracy theories over Kennedy's assassination, her relationship with Ruby—whatever it was—caused her to be viewed with suspicion. Rumors swirled throughout the newspapers, congressional committees, and the public. Rumors about Ruby, of drug deals with Cuba, of Ruby's known acquaintances. As always, "trouble seemed to follow her around."

Parole was difficult for her. The stipulation prohibiting working in places serving alcohol effectively ended her dancing career. She claimed that several attempts were made to set her up for a parole violation and return to prison during the four years after her release.

She was eventually busted again for marijuana possession in Brownwood, Texas. Officers entered her home with a search warrant while she was away and claimed to have found shoeboxes containing small fragments of plants. The "evidence" was sent to Texas Department of Public Safety labs for analysis. In the middle of the search, Candy came home and was arrested.[5]

She was immediately released on $10,000 bail, and the charges were eventually dismissed after two years of haggling in court.

On June 12, 1967, she received a full pardon. She claimed it came as a complete surprise to her—a somewhat startling revelation since pardons require applications and complicated, intricate political maneuvering. If so, her pardon certainly adds fuel to the claims that her original drug bust was a political setup.

Three and a half years of Texas prison time had not broken Candy Barr. But she emerged from the Goree Unit a far different woman than had arrived that day in 1959 wisecracking about wanting a brick house. In the ensuing years she would give occasional interviews, but for the most part she has disappeared from the public's sight and thoughts.

The June 1967 *Oui Magazine* issue carried an interview and seven pictorial pages of her at age forty-one—some photos completely in the buff. *Oui* marketed her interview and photo layout as "the sexiest grandmother we've ever met." She marketed it as giving her a chance to tell her story. That issue today is the most sought-after and expensive back-issue in the magazine's history.

She remains today a Texan icon—recognized not only in her home state but around the country. As the millenium approached and lists were assembled, her name began reappearing again.

The December 1999 issue of *Texas Monthly* proclaimed her "Bad Girl of the Century." "In the early fifties a nymphet with tropical green eyes and a body that would stop the Dow Jones taught the puritans of Dallas the pleasures of sex, and they taught her their version of justice," the magazine declared.[6]

On the national level, the December 1999 issue of *Playboy* named her to its list of the "100 Sexiest Stars of the Century." Candy Barr was ranked #48 ahead of such contemporary sex symbols as Anna Nicole Smith and Kathy Ireland. More significantly, she was considered by *Playboy* to have been sexier than such famous idols as Sally Rand, Greta Garbo, and Gypsy Rose Lee.

Still, her fame and notoriety of the 1950s did not bring her financial success or happiness. Despite her cockiness during the "fast-track" years in the fifties, the 1959 quote of "I've been old since I was fourteen" comes back as a haunting reminder of the terrible price of fame, especially in her chosen profession and lifestyle.

But never has the Texas prison system seen the likes of an inmate like Juanita Dale Phillips, #153781.

Nor is it ever likely to again.

1   "Candy Bar: Time and Trouble Add Wrinkles, But Figure's Still There," uncited and undated source posted in the Texas Prison Museum, Huntsville, Texas.

2   *Oui Magazine*, June 1976, pg. 112.

3   "15,000 Attend First Prison Rodeo of Season," *Houston Post*, October 3, 1960, pg. 2, section I.

4   "Candy Hopes to Do Work in Social Field," *Houston Chronicle*, April 2, 1963, pg. 6, section I.

5   "Candy Stuck With 2nd Dope Charge," uncited and undated source posted in the Texas Prison Museum, Huntsville, Texas.

6   *Texas Monthly*, December 1999.

Chapter Six

"Chop My Toes Off, But Get Me Out of Here"—Clyde Barrow

While Texas has had its share of notorious outlaws and the Texas prison system has had its share of infamous prisoners, few have enjoyed the notoriety or infamy of Clyde Barrow.

Ironically, of the more famous criminals to be housed in Texas's prisons, Barrow actually spent less time than most—just under two years.

But he made two trips to the Eastham prison unit in the 1930s and even more ironically it was his second trip to the prison, in 1934, that made him one of Texas's most famous gangsters and ex-cons. And that second trip lasted only a couple of hours.

Clyde Chesnut Barrow was born near Telico, a small town in north central Texas, on March 24, 1909. When he was a teenager his family moved to West Dallas in 1922. One of several children—some sources say seven, others nine—he matured in the crime-ridden and poverty stricken West Dallas area along the Trinity River flats. In a period where many able-bodied men were unable to find employment, Barrow quickly learned that petty crime paid better than standing in unemployment lines.

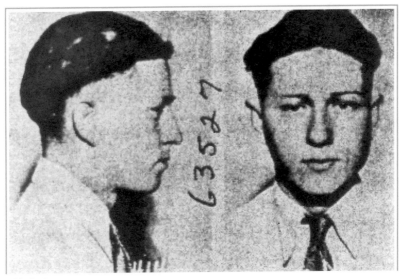

Clyde Barrow

During those formative years, he dropped out of school but learned at least some shade-tree mechanic skills hanging around his father's service station. His first serious run-in with the law, on the record books at least, was in 1926 while he was still a teenager.

At that time he appeared to have settled down somewhat—especially in comparison to his older brother Buck, who most acquaintances and law officers expected to end up in prison soon. Clyde, however, was working full time, had a girlfriend, and was making plans to get married. This seemingly "responsible" period of his life ended with a fight with his financée.

After the fight, she went to the East Texas town of Broddus to visit relatives, leaving Barrow behind in Dallas. Anxious to smooth over the tiff, he talked her mother into joining him in driving to Broddus to convince her to return home.

The trip to Broddus had all the appearances of legitimacy: An automobile was legally rented, and his fiancée's mother accompanied him on the trip. The problem was Barrow had failed to notify the rental company that he was taking the car out of town, and when he didn't return it immediately and they couldn't find him, they filed auto theft charges against him.

Through Barrow's mother, law enforcement officers learned of his trip to Broddus, and when the police tried to arrest him at the house of his fiancée's relatives, he hid out and later escaped.

The police confiscated the rental car and returned it to Dallas, his girlfriend's mother effectively convinced her daughter to break off with this "future criminal," and Clyde ended up hitchhiking back to Dallas where he was arrested for auto theft. The car rental agency, expecting the worst, was happy to get the automobile back and dropped charges against Barrow, but the incident left him a marked man, or in this case, marked boy, in Dallas.

For the next four years the Dallas cops watched him closely. Barrow gave them plenty to observe during that period. By then his older brother Buck had developed into a career criminal, and Clyde was running with him and joining in a string of robberies in and around Dallas.

Then, in 1930, Clyde and Buck ran out of luck during a robbery of a service station in Denton. When Clyde crashed the getaway car, Buck and a third thief were arrested. Clyde escaped but his brother was seriously wounded by gunshot and later sentenced to five years in the state penitentiary.

Clyde made his way back to Dallas, where he met a restaurant waitress and immediately fell in love. This time the relationship would grow and endure the coming trials and tribulations of Clyde Barrow. The waitress' name was Bonnie Parker.

Almost immediately they moved in together, and Barrow was arrested at her home in February of 1930 and charged with the Denton robbery. Despite the fact he was driving the getaway car after a crime that netted his brother five years in prison, Clyde somehow avoided a conviction. His past caught up with him, however.

After he was transported from Denton to Waco, the authorities there did manage to get convictions for burglary and auto theft, and Clyde was sentenced to two years in prison for seven counts. But the sentence was handed down to run concurrently, meaning he ended up with only two years to serve in prison. Compared to Buck's five years in addition to being shot up, Clyde seemed to be leading a charmed life as a petty criminal.

He seemed bent on self-destruction, however, even at that early age. Up to this point most of Clyde Barrow's crimes were not considered particularly violent: burglary, auto theft, avoiding arrest. But at the Waco jail this pattern changed.

Despite the judge's leniency, he feared a trip to the state penitentiary. Bonnie, who had followed him to Denton and then to Waco, agreed to a plan in which she would smuggle a pistol into the jail.

Bonnie Parker, although just nineteen years old, was no angel. She had been previously married to a criminal and had a tattoo "Roy and Bonnie" etched on one of her thighs—an act considered scandalous by "proper society" in the 1920s.

She has been described as attractive but crude and extremely "loud and foul mouthed." At four foot ten and eighty-five pounds, she was petite—almost dainty. A few years later, after she had walked up to a dying motorcycle policeman and calmly rolled him over with her foot before nearly blowing his head off with a shotgun, Texas Ranger Frank Hamer would characterize her: "She was—begging your pardon—a bit of a lady dog."

But in Waco, in 1930, she was just a former waitress hanging around the jail visiting her newly convicted boyfriend.

Although no angel in 1930, she was also not a criminal—at least not a big-time criminal. Not, that is, until she agreed to sneak the pistol into jail and aid Clyde Barrow's escape.

The plan worked, Clyde escaped, and Bonnie left Waco. Clyde was arrested a week later and returned to jail where the judge—not in such a lenient mood after an armed jailbreak—re-sentenced him to the full fourteen years.

If Clyde Barrow had been apprehensive about spending two years in the state penitentiary earlier, he was now terrified at spending fourteen years among the hardened convicts. He had reason to be terrified.

Over the years Clyde Barrow has attained a mythical image as a gutsy badman. There is no question that, with a gun in his hand, he was ruthless, cold-blooded, and vicious. But without a gun in his hand, Clyde Barrow knew he would be a potential victim in Texas's mean prisons.

At five foot seven and weighing only 130 pounds, he knew that in prison he would be the target of Texas's notorious building tenders—inmates given special favors by the guards in exchange for maintaining control over the other inmates. With his small physical stature, Barrow realized he would likely be the victim of sexual advances from one or several of these tough, violently brutal building tenders, especially if he ended up on one of the notorious "work farms."

Another factor causing him concern from within the prison system was the fact that Buck had successfully escaped the Texas Department of Corrections in 1930, and Clyde figured some of the vengeance and retaliation of prison officials and guards might be directed at him once he was committed. He knew, too, that his armed escape from the Waco jail would be a factor in his assignment once he was in prison.

And so, as he sat in jail at Waco awaiting transfer to the prison at Huntsville, Clyde Barrow hardly fit his later image as a fearless outlaw.

The Texas prison system in 1930 was in turmoil. Inmate killings, misappropriation of funds, escapes, charges of brutality, and barbaric living conditions for convicts had been the topic of newspaper columns and legislative debates for several years when Lee Simmons was appointed the director of the prison system on March 25.

Stemming the epidemic of escapes became one of Simmons' priorities, and to that end he began rehiring some of the former prison guards and managers previously released because of brutality charges. While Simmons did, publicly at least, advocate eliminating cruel and brutal treatment of convicts, he also tightened security by creating an atmosphere of fear based in part on discipline and in part on "choppin' cotton," a euphemism for hard labor.

As a result, prison units became work farms under his administration. To stem the tide of escapes, he designated two prison farms as "high security" units. The prison headquarters remained at Huntsville, but the two farms earmarked for escapees or potential escapees were established at the prison farms called Retrieve and Eastham.

Retrieve, a farm unit located on the Texas Gulf Coast near Angleton, was basically a cotton plantation serviced by convicts living and working under brutal conditions. Eastham, also staffed by hardened criminals, was located forty miles north of Huntsville between Trinity and Crockett. Both units were located five to seven miles from the nearest highway and well away from communities of any size. Simmons made sure both units were staffed by veteran guards, farm managers, and wardens and that escape attempts were dealt with promptly and effectively. Despite his public stance against sanctioned brutality by guards, rumors continued to circulate about "spot killings" or inmate deaths resulting from escape "attempts."

The Eastham unit was located in East Texas on approximately 13,000 acres, and prisoners were separated into two work camps. Camp One, the more established work camp, had stone buildings, an infamous "hole," or solitary, and was located in a wooded section of the prison farm. From Camp One, inmate work gangs often were sent out on timber cutting assignments. It had a reputation as a deadly and bloody camp.

Prison Camp Two was located in a separate area of the prison farm and was more temporary in nature. The buildings were wooden and there was no solitary confinement "hole," but the camp had, instead, a sheetmetal "sweatbox" for punishment. Convicts assigned to the sweatbox were forced to stand inside under the hot summer Texas sun. Camp Two also differed from the first camp in that it was located out in the open, away from all trees.

The second camp used work gangs for agricultural production of corn and other farm crops. The primary crop, however, was cotton, and during "pickin' season" the inmates worked what they called "eight hour days—eight in the morning, eight in the evening."[1] Inmates who didn't pick their allotment were often beaten, placed in the sweatbox overnight, or denied food and water until they caught up with the other convicts in the field.

Because Camp Two was located in the center of open, unsheltered agricultural fields, escape was considered almost impossible.

On April 21, 1930, Clyde Barrow was scheduled to be transferred from jail to the penitentiary at Huntsville. During the spring and early summer he was housed at the Huntsville unit awaiting transfer orders to one of the prison work farms. Because he had an armed escape from the Waco jail on his record, Clyde Barrow knew that he would likely be assigned to the Eastham unit. And it terrified him.

One of the reasons he wasn't transferred that summer was that several towns and communities were subpoenaing him to appear in court. These "bench warrants" resulted in no new additional charges against him but did effectively keep him out of the broiling Eastham work camps that summer.

Then his luck ran out. He was transferred to the dreaded "'Ham" and assigned to Prison Camp Two.

During one of those bench warrants, Clyde Barrow had met another convict named Ralph Fults. Years later Fults gave a detailed, but generally unsubstantiated, account of his and Barrow's time in prison in a book titled *Running with Bonnie and Clyde—The Ten Fast Years of Ralph Fults.*

Fults, who would later run with Clyde Barrow during the "Bonnie and Clyde" gangster period, claimed that Barrow held his own in the Eastham cotton fields. He claimed that on one occasion a guard tried to run Barrow over with his horse in a cotton row only to have the small-statured Clyde sidestep and grab the reins and draw the horse to a stop. Fults also reported that after a "stare down" Barrow and the guard backed away from each other.[2] Given the fact that guards rarely, if ever, backed down from a confrontation with a convict—it was seen as a challenge to their authority—it is doubtful that the event unfolded as Fults described it. At the very least, Clyde Barrow would have received a beating or at least a lash across the face from the guard's reins—overly long leather straps that usually had a tight knot braided or tied into the end to serve as a whip.

Fults also reported that at one point he and Barrow attempted to kill an inmate "snitch" by felling a tree on him during a timber clearing work gang assignment. Speculating that Barrow was then transferred to Camp One in an effort to separate the two, Fults was separated from Clyde but continued to occasionally talk with him when work gangs from the two camps met in the fields.

It was while Barrow was assigned to Camp One that Fults claims the future gangleader killed his first man. It is not an accepted story, and prison archives do not substantiate it, but Fults' story does shed light on what must have been a daily survival concern for the five-foot-seven, 130-pound Clyde Barrow.

Considered small for a man in almost any situation, Barrow especially stood out in the usually large, tough prison population. While at Camp One, according to Fults' unsubstantiated claim, Barrow was being sexually assaulted and "turned out" by a particularly brutal building tender. According to this story, a third convict—also a building tender and a lifer—plotted with Clyde to kill the antagonizer. Clyde, supposedly offering himself as bait in the toilets, used a lead pipe to kill the sexual predator by clubbing him in the head. The second building tender, knowing his life sentence couldn't be made more severe, then plunged a knife in the dead inmate's body and claimed the killing.[3]

Clyde Barrow, in this scheme, was then rid of his attacker and the other building tender continued his life sentence free of the predator. This story was certainly possible, and no doubt similar attacks did occur over the years involving various inmates, but Texas prison records don't substantiate Fults' claim with regards to this one. It was—and is—a common practice for weaker inmates to claim stories of killing to enhance themselves in the eyes of their fellow inmates.

The alleged killing of the building tender supposedly occurred during 1931. By December of that year Buck Barrow, still an escapee from the Texas prison system, surrendered himself and returned to Huntsville where he was assigned light duty due to an injury.

The Barrow family had already been petitioning for a pardon for Clyde, and with his brother's show of "good faith" by voluntarily returning, the momentum for Clyde's release picked up. But not fast enough for Clyde—still struggling daily to survive on the "Bloody 'Ham."

Other than death, parole, or discharge, about the only way an inmate could get off Eastham was a medical transfer, and self-mutilations were common in both work camps. Finally, in desperation, Clyde convinced another inmate to chop off two of his toes with an axe.

Fults would later claim it was Clyde's burning desire to be reunited with Buck in Huntsville that precipitated this action. Most authorities probably felt it was just another desperate, self-serving act by an inmate not man enough to take daily work and life on the 'Ham.

On January 27, 1932, Clyde Barrow was admitted to the hospital clinic at Huntsville with two toes of his left foot completely severed. He must have been dismayed when the prison officials bandaged him up and sent him back to Eastham. The self-mutilation had failed to get Clyde Barrow off the dreaded unit.

Ironically, as he was still healing from the loss of his toes, he received word from Huntsville that a pardon had been approved for him, and on February 2, 1932, he was released after serving twenty-three months of the original two-year sentence.

After just two years in the Texas prison system he was released back onto the streets and into the arms of Bonnie Parker. He swore he would never return to prison even if he had to die resisting.

But he didn't keep his promise, at least not completely. Almost exactly two years after his release, Clyde Barrow would return to Eastham's Camp One. But this would be a two-hour visit that would eventually lead to his death, and also that of Bonnie Parker.

But a lot happened, and happened fast, to Clyde and Bonnie in the two years before his return to Eastham.

Ralph Fults had received a conditional pardon some five months before Clyde Barrow, and in the early months of 1932 the two ex-cons reunited and were joined by another of Clyde's old acquaintances from his West Dallas days: Raymond Hamilton.

Clyde Barrow, even after his horrendous experiences at Eastham, seemed more intent than ever to follow a path of crime and violence, and with his new associates including Bonnie Parker, they carried out a series of violent holdups. His gang activities for the next year and a half captivated the American public and press as they went on a crime spree that read like something out of a Hollywood scriptwriter's imagination.

On March 22, 1932, the gang committed a bank robbery at Kaufman, and somehow Bonnie was caught and jailed. On April 28 Clyde and a woman never identified robbed the Bucher Grocery at Hillsboro and, in the process, killed the owner. Most historians consider this murder to be Clyde Barrow's first killing, not the unsubstantiated building tender incident at Eastham. At the time, Bonnie Parker was still in jail at Kaufman, but on June 17, 1932, she was released and rejoined Barrow. In the coming months she would more than make up for what she had missed in the robbery and killing at Hillsboro.

In early August 1932 Barrow, Hamilton, and Parker were in Atoka, Oklahoma, at a dance when Clyde and Raymond Hamilton got into a fight and a drunken Bonnie Parker attacked a deputy sheriff trying to intervene. As the group was leaving, both the deputy and the sheriff were killed by gunfire.

In mid-August Barrow and Parker kidnapped a police officer in Carlsbad and dropped him off in San Antonio the next day. A fascinated American public continued to follow the unfolding saga of Bonnie and Clyde.

In September, with Raymond Hamilton still in the group, they committed a string of bank robberies as far north as Michigan. At that time Hamilton left the pair and was later captured, returned to Texas, and sentenced to 263 years in prison. He almost immediately was returned to the dreaded Eastham unit.

Barrow and Parker continued their crime spree. On October 11 they robbed the Hall Grocery in Sherman and killed the owner. On December 5, 1932, they attempted another of the auto "switches" they were already famous for in Temple and, in the process, killed Doyle Johnson, who tried to stop the auto theft.

Only one month later, on January 6 of 1933, they killed Deputy Sheriff Malcolm Davis in Dallas during an attempted ambush by law officers. After the Dallas killing Clyde and Bonnie left Texas because of the intense manhunt.

Sometime in February 1933 a National Guard armory in Missouri was robbed, and several .30-caliber Browning (BAR) automatic rifles and Colt .45-caliber automatic pistols were reported missing. Some of those weapons would later be traced to Clyde Barrow.

On April 13, 1933, Joplin, Missouri Constable J.W. Harryman and Detective Harry McGinnis were killed and a Missouri Highway Patrolman wounded in a shoot-out while investigating complaints of loud partying by a group of four people. In a hail of automatic weapons fire, the group escaped again but left behind a poem written by Bonnie Parker and a roll of film. When developed, the film provided a "scrapbook" of Bonnie and Clyde including one photo that was destined to become the symbol of Bonnie Parker. In it, she had one foot on the getaway car bumper, a large pistol in one hand, and a cigar in her mouth.

June 11, 1933, they wrecked their car near Wellington, Oklahoma, and wounded a woman trying to help them. Responding to the wreck, two Oklahoma law officers were captured, handcuffed together around a tree, stripped down to their underwear, and wrapped in barbed wire. Two days later they were found suffering from exposure and dehydration but later recovered.

Less than two weeks later Barrow and Parker robbed a grocery in Fayetteville, Arkansas, and in their getaway shot and killed an unarmed town marshal. At this point, except for the auto wreck, the couple had seemed almost untouchable in their deadly crime spree.

On June 28, 1933, their luck held out but began to falter in Platte City, Missouri, when local police surrounded them. Again, they escaped in a hail of gunfire, but this time Buck Barrow was killed and his wife captured and both Clyde and Bonnie were seriously wounded.

For the remainder of 1933 they disappeared while they recuperated from their wounds.

When they resurfaced, it would be at Barrow's second—and last—trip to Eastham and the Texas Department of Corrections. Actually, that final trip occurred during two days.

Raymond Hamilton, who had been shipped from Huntsville to Eastham's Camp One earlier, had slipped word to Clyde Barrow requesting help in escaping. Clyde was probably intrigued with the idea more out of a desire to hit back at the prison system that had been so brutal to him than out of friendship to Hamilton.

On January 14, 1934, Clyde Barrow and Bonnie Parker delivered Hamilton's brother, Floyd, and another ex-con named James Mullens to a point on a dirt road near the Eastham Camp One just before sunrise.

Mullens and Hamilton hiked near the camp and hid two army-issue Colt .45 automatic pistols packed inside a piece of rubber tire inner tube. It was a Sunday morning.

Two days later, on January 16, Clyde returned with Bonnie and Mullens around 6:00 A.M. Leaving Bonnie in the getaway car, the two men positioned themselves in a wooded area near the field where they knew Raymond Hamilton's work squad would be assigned that morning.

This incident, as in almost every aspect of Clyde Barrow's adult life, has been reported so many times and in so many ways that the facts seem to blur. Even accounts by writers who are generally considered "reliable" do not always agree on just how that morning unraveled.

One account, published years later in a book titled *Assignment Huntsville: Memoirs of a Texas Prison Official*,[4] is generally considered the most credible report. The author, Lee Simmons, was the general manager of the prison system at the time.

Simmons reported that about two hundred prisoners were cutting timber near a country road that morning when Raymond Hamilton "jumped" squads—moved over into another work squad where he was not assigned.

Ralph Fults later claimed that the mounted guard, named Olan Bozeman, had called Major M.H. Crowson over to watch as Hamilton was to be whipped for the infraction. Lee Simmons claimed that Crowson was only called over as a backup security officer.

Major Crowson was an excellent marksman who was assigned as a "long-arm man" or "backfield man." In later years the prison would refer to these solitary guards as "high riders." Their duty was to remain well away from the inmates, even out of sight, and shoot any convict attempting to "run" from a work squad.

As such, Crowson was grossly negligent in riding up to Officer Bozeman and Hamilton that morning. It was a mistake that cost him and Bozeman their lives.

As Crowson rode up, Raymond Hamilton and another convict named Joe Palmer came around from behind a brush pile, firing away with the automatic Colt .45s that had been hidden there two days earlier. As the officers' horses bucked the wounded men to the ground, Clyde Barrow and James Mullins opened fire with machine guns, scattering the remaining guards and prisoners.

Hamilton and Palmer were joined by two other convicts named Henry Methvin and Hilton Bybee as they ran from the scene, leaving Bozeman mortally wounded and Crowson dead at the scene. As they ran through the early morning light, Bonnie Parker sat in the getaway car, honking the horn as a beacon.

During the two years Clyde Barrow had been in prison and especially during the period he had been assigned to Eastham's notorious Camp One, he must have dreamed often of an armed escape. On January 16, 1934, the armed escape he carried out was successful even beyond his wildest dreams.

Simmons later directly held Major Crowson responsible for the success of the raid because he broke the "backfield rider" rules and came within the perimeter of the work squad. "Had he kept his post on the edge of the timber, things would have turned out differently, I have no doubt," Simmons later wrote.[5]

While Clyde Barrow's final visit to Eastham was a success—at least from his perspective—it ultimately led to his downfall.

An embarrassed and revengeful manager of the prison system, Lee Simmons swore personal revenge for Crowson's death and the escape of four convicts that morning.

To that end, he enlisted the aid of a former Texas Ranger named Frank Hamer. Hamer had resigned from the rangers in protest of the political corruption during the Ferguson administrations, but Simmons managed to get Governor "Ma" Ferguson and her husband to approve Hamer as a Special Investigator for the Texas Prison System. At this point the death warrants of Clyde Barrow and Bonnie Parker had begun to be executed. Bonnie and Clyde had exactly 102 days left to live.

Of all the vast literature on Bonnie and Clyde, Frank Hamer is generally considered *the* authority on the period leading to their deaths. After the ambush in Bienville Parish, Louisiana, that resulted in the death of both Barrow and Parker on May 24, 1934, Hamer later granted an interview to Dr. Walter Prescott Webb, who was writing what would eventually become the "Bible" of Texas Ranger books: *The Texas Rangers: A Century of Frontier Defense*.[6] Because many of the participants in the Bonnie and Clyde saga were still alive in 1935, Hamer did not list any sources for his interview with Webb and never publicly commented on the pair again before his death in 1955.

In 1968 John H. Jenkins and H. Gordon Frost were allowed access to Hamer's private files and published a book titled *"I'm Frank Hamer": The Life of a Texas Peace Officer*.[7] That account, based upon Hamer's personal files and the 1934 interview with Webb, have resulted in *"I'm Frank Hamer"* being considered by many historians and authorities as the only authentic and accurate account of the final days of Bonnie and Clyde.

Despite the fact they were cold-blooded killers, time has somehow elevated Bonnie and Clyde to American folk heroes. Clyde Barrow's armed raid on Eastham's Camp One in 1934 was the first of its kind in Texas prison history and remains today one of the most dramatic escapes ever carried out.

This photo is purported to have been taken in the dorm at Eastham where Clyde Barrow was incarcerated. Some historians claim Barrow murdered a "Building Tender" behind one of the rear concrete posts in the center of the photo but no prison records verify it. (photo source: Texas State Archives, courtesy of Jester III Unit, Texas Department of Criminal Justice).

1   Phillips, John Neal, *Running with Bonnie and Clyde—The Ten Fast Years of Ralph Fults* (Norman and London: University of Oklahoma Press, 1996), pg. 37.

2   Ibid., pg. 50.

3   Ibid., pp. 52-4.

4   Simmons, Lee, *Assignment Huntsville: Memoirs of a Texas Prison Official* (Austin: University of Texas Press, 1959).

5   Ibid., pg. 117.

6   Webb, Walter Prescott, *The Texas Rangers: A Century of Frontier Defense* (Austin: University of Texas Press, 1935).

7   Frost, H. Gordon and John Jenkins, *"I'm Frank Hamer": The Life of a Texas Peace Officer* (Austin: Pemberton Press, 1969).

Chapter Seven

"The Huntsville Prison Tigers"— Showdown at Houston's Buff Stadium

During the summer of 1935, America slogged along in the depths of the Great Depression while in Texas, Houston sweltered in heat, humidity, mosquitoes, and baseball.

The 1930s were premier years for professional baseball in Houston. The city had finally received a professional Texas League baseball team—the Houston Buffalos—and Buff Stadium had been built southeast of downtown in 1928. That year the Buffs won the Texas League championship and the Dixie Series (a tournament between the Texas League champion and the Southern League champion).

In 1930 lights were installed at the stadium and a tradition of baseball was started in Houston that lasts to this day and includes the Buffs, the Colt .45s, and the Astros.

But 1935 was the banner year for baseball during that decade. Major League names like Dizzy Dean and Joe Medwick had already passed through the Buff organization on the way to the parent club—the St. Louis Cardinals. Current players on the roster were considered sure bets to make the big leagues soon.

As a city, Houston had been spared some of the financial disaster created by the Depression, due in part to the ship channel positioned just east of the baseball stadium.

That was part of the ambiance of Buff Stadium during the summer of 1935: ship channel odors intermingling with the smell of fresh-baked bread from the nearby Fair Maid Bakery. Ninety-degree heat combined with ninety-percent humidity to create a perfect environment for large roving black swarms of Gulf Coast mosquitoes. Behind right field, engineers would direct train whistles at the players as they passed.

The Houston Buffalos started the season off with an early exhibition game in Huntsville. Behind the high walls of the Huntsville unit, the professional Buffs took on a team of convict prisoners known as the Huntsville Prison Tigers. It was no contest—the Buffs won handily by the score of 28-0. The score was reported in the *Houston Post* but was barely noticed in the excitement of starting the 1935 Texas League season for real.

Most fans simply noted—and dismissed—the Huntsville Prison Tigers that spring. But behind those ominous, tall penitentiary walls, the team regrouped for their coming season that included, obviously, all home games.

But in many ways they played a pivotal role in Texas baseball during the summer of 1935. Their season became, in a sense, the story of two cities—Brehnam and Huntsville—and a collision course that would end explosively at Houston on September 8 at Buff Stadium.

In today's commercialized sports world, the semi-pro baseball teams of Texas in 1935 probably seem like an anachronism to many. Financially strapped Texans were entertainment hungry during the 1930s, and baseball was often the only affordable show in town. Almost every town of any size

1935 Huntsville Prison Tigers. All of their games that year were "home" games except one. At Houston's Buff Stadium they swept a double-header from the semi-pro champions from Brenham. (photo courtesy of Texas State Archives)

had a semi-pro team consisting of local boys hoping to be noticed and earn a ticket to the big leagues.

Usually sponsored by local businesses, the players received little if any salary and certainly no perks as do players today. As a result, the play on the field was truly a labor of love for the game: Contests were hard fought, and players went all out all the time. Texas semi-pro was, in short, simply some of the purest, best, hardest played, no-holds-barred baseball in Texas—if not the world—in 1935.

And Texas towns loved their teams. Because the players were local, they were daily heroes to the kids. Mayoral politics revolved around player endorsements. Businesses closed for afternoon home games. Semi-pro baseball teams in many Texas towns were virtually the focal point of the community. Large cities like Houston had several teams, and some of them were powerhouses. In 1935 the Houston Grand Prize team was expected to sweep through their season and easily win the state championship.

The small town of Brenham, northwest of Houston, had a semi-pro team named the Brenham Sun Oilers. It was an established team with good, solid players. The Sun Oilers played a formidable schedule every year and 1935 was no exception. But it was also a year in which the community of Brenham anticipated a semi-pro state championship for the Sun Oilers at the annual fall *Houston Post* state tournament.

The *Post* tournament may have been, in 1935, the premier semi-professional baseball series anywhere—not just in baseball-crazy Texas. Heavily scouted by the major and minor leagues, the tournament usually yielded some tentative contracts to outstanding players. By the mid-thirties the tournament had become so big that only one stadium in Texas could hold it: Houston's Buff Stadium.

Semi-pro teams took on all comers during that period. Usually the schedules revolved around nearby towns, creating fierce rivalries. Other times the teams would solicit and play nearby college teams. In central and southeast Texas, many of the teams would also play prison baseball teams. The Central Unit and Ramsey Unit prison teams routinely played local semi-pro teams with some success.

The main prison unit in Texas however was located at Huntsville, where prison director Lee Simmons and Huntsville manager Albert Moore had developed a team named the Prison Tigers. Both Moore and Simmons were avid baseball fans and challenged all comers, with the provision that the games had to be played on the baseball field inside the prison unit.

The Prison Tigers didn't just challenge semi-pro teams; after all, the Houston Buffalos had visited to start the 1935 exhibition season. Despite the humiliating and devastating 28-0 loss to the visiting Buffs, Moore and Simmons continued to groom and train the Prison Tigers that spring and summer. Seven of their scheduled games that year were with the highly respected Brenham Sun Oilers.

But except for a few local newspaper reports, the Huntsville Prison Tigers pretty much faded from the public eye after their 28-0 loss to the Houston Buffs that spring.

The Brenham Sun Oilers played their way through a particularly tough schedule during that summer. Playing good, solid baseball against established top-notch opponents, they slowly built a good—but not dominating—record. By early September they qualified for the *Houston Post* semi-pro championship tournament. They were not considered favorites to win: The odds-makers in 1935 were favoring Houston's own Grand Prize team.

The Brenham Sun Oilers and the Huntsville Prison Tigers played seven times in Huntsville during that summer. The final results were a dead draw: three wins for each team and one eleven-inning tie. The visiting teams (and they were *all* visiting teams) at Huntsville complained about the less than state-of-the-art baseball facilities inside the penitentiary but accepted them as part of the program. Someone once described the prison playing field as a "baseball field with thirty-foot outfield walls and 'extra' outfielders carrying guns." Still, despite their obvious "home field advantage," the Prison Tigers were considered formidable baseball opponents.

Obviously, baseball games inside the Huntsville prison were big events for the convicts. A stadium was constructed and included a stand for the seven-man convict band, which spiritedly cheered on the "local" players.

Simmons and Moore had procured real baseball uniforms for the convicts—not stripped suits—and their equipment was at least adequate. A baseball game inside the Huntsville unit was, for all practical purposes, a true baseball game, and the quality of play was excellent. The one thing Simmons and Moore didn't have with the Prison Tigers was validation. Simmons, especially, longed for the showdown that would give his convicts the opportunity to truly establish themselves and prison baseball in Texas.

Despite the rough loss to the Houston Buffs to open the season, the Prison Tigers earned a very respectable 25-8 record that summer for a .758 winning percentage. And they didn't run up numbers on easy teams.

The Prison Tigers fielded a truly "Texan" team that summer, notwithstanding the fact that four of the starters were convicted burglars, three were forgers, and two were serving time for auto theft.

The team's success revolved around the pitching of Buford "Army" Armstrong and the powerful slugging of Carl Littlejohn.

Armstrong, from Dallas, had developed a reputation as a "speedball merchant," and the Prison Tigers' fortunes seemed to be based on his performances. Armstrong had been, in the words of Lee Simmons, "a hard case, but he had been coming around fairly well of late." In July of 1935 a convict was killed in the Huntsville unit, and Armstrong was sent to a "hard-time" farm unit while the investigation was being conducted. During this period the Prison Tigers lost the next two games they played. Armstrong was quickly "cleared" and returned to the team, and the Prison Tigers started winning again.

ACE OF PRISONERS

Here is "Army" Armstrong, speed ball merchant of the Texas Prison Tigers, who this afternoon at 2:30 at Buffalo stadium will face the Brenham Sun Oilers, winners of the Houston Post's state championship semi-pro tournament.

This September 8, 1935 *Houston Post* photograph is one of the few pictures of a Huntsville Prison Tiger player in which the player is named.

The *Houston Chronicle* characterized Armstrong as a "black-haired fireball hurler" and "the strong right arm" of the Prison Tigers. He "relied mostly on a burning fastball and for a change of pace mixed in one still faster."[1]

Carl Littlejohn was the first baseman and also an accomplished ball player before that 1935 season. In fact, he was no stranger to Houston baseball fans, having starred on the 1928 Houston Buffalo team that won the Texas League and defeated Birmingham in the Dixie Series.

After those championships, Littlejohn had gotten into an automobile and driven away from Houston. Unfortunately it wasn't his car, and in 1935 he was playing first base for the Prison Tigers and serving time for auto theft. He led the Prison Tigers that summer with a batting average of .380. Besides being the team's power hitter, he also pitched in relief of Armstrong.

Raymond McNurlen caught Armstrong that summer. He was described as "a big fellow but moves around satisfactorily for his size." He was sentenced to prison out of Breckenridge, Texas.

Joining Littlejohn in the infield were Amarillo native Howard "Brigham" Young at second and Jose Esparza at shortstop. Esparza was a Mexican citizen but was listed as from "Huntsville" on the team program. During the course of the summer the *Post* would variously refer to him as "peppery," "Chilli," and "fiery." Playing third base was Earl Holbrook from Dallas whom the *Post* referred to as the "stocky" third baseman and "one of the best fielding third sackers to be seen in action in these parts in several years."[2]

Playing right field was a player listed as "Big" Dalton and at other times as "Lefty." The *Post* classified him as "everything but a finished fielder, but his big bat carries a tremendous wallop."

Center field was covered by Lawrence Guinn, a Houstonian, whom the *Post* called "a ballhawk of the first water." His field play was characterized as "covering the vast area of center field like a blanket and base runners hesitated to take liberties with his throwing arm." Guinn was also a left-handed hitter known for his extra-base hits.

Another Houstonian, Arthur McCann, played left field with "no flash but good, consistent brand of baseball."

With this roster, it was obvious why the Prison Tigers had a .758 winning percentage during 1935.

On August 18 the *Houston Post* reported that Brenham had come from behind with two runs in the top of the ninth to beat the Prison Tigers. The convict team had placed runners on second and third with no outs in the bottom of the ninth but could not get the ball out of the infield for the next three batters.[3]

Almost every game the Prison Tigers played, it seemed, was hotly contested. On August 22 the *Post* reported on a double-header in which the Prison Tigers swept Lufkin 7-1 and 10-3. In the first game Armstrong hurled a six-hitter "despite the fact the sun was as 'broiling' as a savored steak." Littlejohn was the winning pitcher in the nightcap and hit two home runs. Dalton and Young, the *Post* reported, "continued their rapping while the fiery "Chilli" Esparza remained on the 'sacks' more than a snoozing storekeeper."[4]

On August 26 the powerhouse Shell Oilers of Houston beat the Prison Tigers 4-2 in a "pretty mound duel."

So as August drew to a close in 1935, the Prison Tigers finished a highly successful season behind the high walls of the Huntsville prison unit. But as a convict team, their season was over and all they could do was sit back and listen to professional games on the radio.

In Houston during this period, the field was being assembled for the annual *Houston Post* semi-pro Texas state championship tournament. The teams were quickly scheduled, and the overwhelming favorite to win the tournament—Houston's own Grand Prize—became the early betting favorite.

Slowly the brackets of the tournament chart began to fill up, and when completed the Brenham Sun Oilers had been included.

Brenham had enjoyed a successful but not spectacular season in 1935. As the summer had progressed, they had improved with each game but still were not considered tournament threats that September.

It was a major upset in the making, then, when on September 2 they found themselves playing for the state semi-pro championship against the powerful Conroe team in Buff Stadium.

But back in Huntsville, prison director Lee Simmons had yet another surprise set to be announced after the championship game.

The September 2 tournament final was a classic game with ninth-inning drama on both sides. Going into the ninth tied, Conroe scored two runs to take a seemingly insurmountable lead. The Brenham Sun Oilers, however, rallied as they had all season to score three runs in the bottom of the ninth and win the state championship.[5]

Next to the Houston Buffs, the *Post* tournament was the biggest baseball news in Houston. The September 3 issue of the newspaper ran six-column headlines announcing Brenham's championship. The second line of the headline, however, sprung the biggest surprise of all: "Prison Tigers Play Post Tourney All-Stars Here Sunday."

Prison director Lee Simmons had waited for the tournament conclusion to deliver his well-kept secret. Simmons was a close friend of *Houston Post* sports columnist Lloyd Gregory, and Gregory proceeded to spotlight the Prison Tigers throughout the week preceding the game—scheduled to be an afternoon double-header played not at the Huntsville prison unit, but at Houston Buff Stadium and open to all fans in Houston and the surrounding towns.

Simmons had pulled a classic fast one: Not only was he going to pit his convict ballplayers against semi-pro professional players but he was going to do it in a Buff Stadium packed with "free-world" fans and media. But he was not finished.

The next day, September 4, the *Post* ran another surprise headline: "Brenham Oilers Will Play Prison Tigers Sunday." Lee Simmons, the paper reported, turned down the all-star club. "It's Champs or Nothing," he was quoted.[6]

The effect was electrifying in Houston and throughout Texas. The Buffs were struggling during 1935—September 4 also marked their tenth straight loss, a 5-3 defeat at the hands of the San Antonio Missions. The Brenham Sun Oilers vs. Huntsville Prison Tigers game suddenly became the hottest baseball item in Houston.

Both the *Post* and the *Houston Chronicle* gave considerable coverage to the preparations for the game. On September 5 the *Chronicle* reported that "nine members of the state prison orchestra, led by Bob Silver, the boy bandit once sentenced to death for a theater holdup slaying, will accompany the team to Houston."[7]

Bob Silver seemed to be a well-known name around the Houston area in 1935, and the prison orchestra had a very good reputation, at least in the newspapers. Previously on death row and awaiting execution in Old Sparky, Silver had been saved by executive clemency and had been orchestra leader at Huntsville for the past nine years. He was scheduled to be discharged in 1936 and promised an excellent program at Buff Stadium.

Preparation for the game also took on a high profile in the newspapers. The *Post* reported that a piano for the use of the talented "ivory tickler" in the prison band had been installed in the stadium grandstand for the double-header.

As game day neared, interest and coverage continued to grow. The press box in the stadium was wired so that S.E. Barnett, the manager of the prison print shop, could telephone an account of the game—play-by-play—to the convicts listening back at Huntsville in the prison chapel.

This being the first "road game" for the convict team, there was some concern for security. By now, the Associated Press had picked up the story and on September 5 reported in the *Chronicle* that the team would be made trusties for the trip to Houston. "Manager Moore and Night Warden T.T. Easley will take the boys down in two civilian automobiles," the AP reported. "Moore said he thought Warden Wald would be willing to make trusties of the whole ball club with the exception of two members, 'and you couldn't run those two away.'"[8]

Interest in the game was so great that a crowded stadium was expected. Admission prices were 25 cents for grandstand and bleacher seats and 40 cents for reserved. Twenty percent of the gate receipts would be used to pay for stadium rental, and the remainder of proceeds would be split evenly between the two teams. For the Brenham Sun Oiler players, who were, after all, semi-professional baseball players, it meant at least some pay for playing. For the Prison Tigers team, however, all proceeds were earmarked for the prison recreational fund.

Ernest Goss, manager of the ABC Store in Houston, offered a large basket of fruit and cakes to the first Prison Tiger to score a run in the double-header, otherwise the convict players were simply playing for "love of the game" and the opportunity to legally escape the high walls of the Huntsville prison for an afternoon.

That afternoon, September 8, the stadium began filling up early and *kept* filling up. By game time at 2:30 it was obvious that the attendance would be the largest of the 1935 season in Buff Stadium—including the Houston Buffalos regular season schedule and the *Post* semi-pro state championship tournament.

"Army" Armstrong was scheduled to pitch the first game for the Prison Tigers and Carl Littlejohn was slated to hurl the second game. During the pregame warm-ups, Bob Silver and his orchestra entertained the fans as undercover guards kept wary watch over the players on field and the musicians in the grandstand.

The Prison Tigers were selected as the "home team" for the opener which meant the Brenham Sun Oilers would bat first. The order would be reversed for the second contest.

The first inning of the first game started as a pitcher's duel with neither team scoring. Armstrong also shut out Brenham in the top of the second, and the Prison Tigers took the lead in their half of the inning. Littlejohn singled. A utility player named Eggleston, catching in place of McNurlen, reached first on an error with Littlejohn taking second. "Big" Dalton advanced both runners with a sacrifice bunt, and Littlejohn then scored on Armstrong's long fly to left.

Brenham tied the score at 1-1 in the top of the third on an infield hit, a stolen base, and a single. The Prison Tigers failed to score in the bottom of the third and then the Sun Oilers appeared to break the game open.

In the forth, Brenham scored three runs after two errors by Rivas and Young of the Prison Tigers to open the inning.

Both Armstrong and the Sun Oilers pitcher, named Albers, settled down, and the score remained 4-1 in favor of the Texas semi-professional champion Sun Oilers.

Only six outs away from a victory, it looked like the powerhouse team from Brenham had simply outplayed and outmatched the convict team from Huntsville.

In the bottom of the eighth, however, the Prison Tigers appeared to be staging a rally when Armstrong, Esparza, and

Young singled but scored only one run to trail 4-2 going into the final inning.

Armstrong blanked the Sun Oilers in the top of the ninth, setting up the final chance for the convict team to rally and come from behind.

And, to the delight of the packed crowd, Littlejohn opened by singling to center field. Because of a "game leg," the faster Guinn was allowed to run for him. The pinch-running move paid off when Eggleston doubled to right and Guinn scored—cutting the Sun Oiler lead to 4-3. Dalton, attempting a sacrifice bunt, beat out the throw, and the Prison Tigers had runners on first and third with one out. Brenham brought in a relief pitcher named Kasprowicz. Armstrong then flied out to left, but Eggleston scored to tie the game. Kasprowicz then got the third and final out of the bottom of the ninth, but the damage had been done and the game was going into extra innings.

Armstrong, despite allowing four runs, had pitched a superb game for the Prison Tigers. Again he blanked the Sun Oilers in the top of the tenth, giving him six straight innings of shutout pitching from the fifth to the tenth. He would finish the game with five strikeouts and one walk credited to his statistics that afternoon.

With Bob Silver's prison orchestra playing, the crowd was literally stomping and screaming in their seats. As the Sun Oilers took the field in the bottom of the tenth, two policemen approached prison director Lee Simmons near the Prison Tigers dugout.

"What about this collection?" one of the officers asked Simmons.

"What collection?"

"There are a couple of fellows taking up a collection for the prison orchestra," one of the officers replied.

"Grab 'em and take the money away from them," Simmons shouted. The officers responded by arresting the two " collectors" who turned out to be ex-convicts trying to cash in on the Prison Tiger's popularity with the crowd that afternoon.[9] The *Chronicle* also later reported that after good plays by the prison team, coins would be tossed onto the playing field.

The Prison Tigers entered the bottom of the tenth inning knowing that the state champion Sun Oilers could not be contained indefinitely and that they had to rally soon to claim the game.

"Chilli" Esparza opened the inning by grounding to short but advanced to second base on a throwing error. As the acknowledged "speedster" on the Prison Tigers, he presented a dangerous threat to score on even a shallow fly ball. "Brigham" Young attempted to advance him with a sacrifice bunt but popped up to the Brenham pitcher for the first out.

Lawrence Guinn, the "ballhawk of the first water," then stepped to the plate for the Prison Tigers. As the drama heightened, the crowd silenced. Kasprowicz wound and pitched: ball one. Guinn dug into the batter's box for the second pitch: ball two.

Any thoughts that Kasprowicz might be intentionally pitching around Guinn disappeared when the third pitch curved in for a called strike. The count was 2-1 when the next pitch, a blazing fastball, caught the corner for the second strike to even the count. Without winding, Kasprowicz came into the plate with another fastball—this one barely missing the strike zone.

Guinn, who had yet to swing the bat, found himself in the classic baseball scenario: extra innings, runner in scoring position, and the count full at 3-2. At second base, Esparza was dancing on top of the bag. Kasprowicz and the Sun Oilers could only speculate as to whether the fleet Mexican would be given the signal to run with the pitch since there was only one out.

This time, as Guinn dug in again, Kasprowicz took a little more time and a little bigger windup. The pitch came in—another fastball. Lee Simmons later reported a "crack" of the bat and Esparza "streaking" for home.

The crowd erupted and when Esparza scored, giving the Prison Tigers an extra-inning victory over the state semi-professional champions of Texas, Bob Silver and the prison orchestra broke into victory music.

After the first game, with its extra-inning heroics, the second billing of the double-header seemed almost anticlimactic. The crowd, however, got another sterling performance from both teams. Carl Littlejohn's "game leg" miraculously healed, and he took the mound for the Prison Tigers and locked up with a Sun Oilers pitcher named Rosenberg in a scoreless pitcher's duel for five innings. Then in the top of the sixth (the Sun Oilers were the "home team" for the second contest)

The Huntsville Prison Tigers team that defeated the Brenham Sun Oilers at Houston's old Buff Stadium in 1935. (photo courtesy of Texas State Library and Archives)

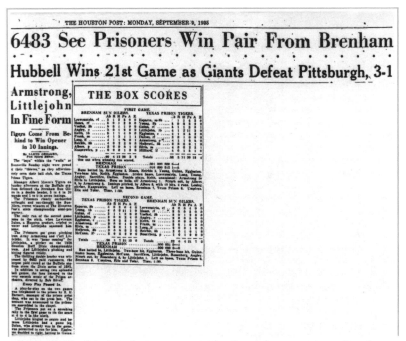

The 1935 double-header victory over the Texas State semi-pro Brenham Sun Oilers was full-page sports headline news for the Huntsville Prison Tigers.

Guinn tripled and later scored when Littlejohn squeezed him home. Littlejohn continued to pitch shutout ball, allowing only four hits, and the Prison Tigers won the second game by a score of 1-0—an abbreviated contest of seven innings due to the extra-inning first game.

Houston's old Buff Stadium is long gone—torn down in the late sixties, but some of the old-time baseball fans there still lament its passing. Buff Stadium was as renowned for its eccentricities as it was for its baseball.

Opened on April 11, 1928, to a capacity crowd of 12,000 fans, the stadium became a symbol of what the game and sport of baseball meant to Texas in the era just before the stock market crash and Depression.

Some of the best baseball in Texas, if not the whole world, was played on the dusty basepaths of Buff Stadium in humidity so heavy it created dew on the outfield grass and in mosquitoes so thick the large electric fans in the bleachers only made them angry.

But Buff Stadium also provided more than excellent baseball for the fans. It also provided entertainment—entertainment not found in professional sports today. After a rain delay in the 1940s, for example, it would not be unusual to see the Buffs president and general manager, Allen Russell, throwing gasoline and matches on the infield to dry out the dirt so the game could resume.

Weatherproofed domed stadiums were unheard of during that era, but Buff Stadium did have what some claim was the first air-conditioned ladies room in baseball. As an oasis in Houston's oppressive heat and humidity, it must have been a highly popular place—a fact borne out by the fact that one Buffs team evicted the ladies to celebrate winning the Dixie League championship.

Fred Ankenman, manager of the team from 1926 to 1942, created a 25-cent admission program for kids. Not 25 cents per game, but 25 cents for a limited *season pass*. Reflecting the Jim Crow segregation of public facilities of that period, Ankenman expanded the program, known as the Houston Knothole Gang, to also include a Colored Knothole Gang.

By 1950 the Houston heat and humidity had become so notorious that the Buffs attempted something unheard of by a professional team in Houston at that time, or since. That summer the Buff players wore their customary wool uniforms but with short pants. The experiment was a flop—the Buffs placed last that year, and the shorts were abandoned for good.

The following year Russell had a hard-throwing left-handed pitcher on the roster named Wilmer Mizell. Wilmer came to Texas from a small Alabama town with an unusual name and a total population of thirty-seven. Russell thought it would be a great promotional stunt to shuttle the entire town of Vinegar Bend, Alabama, to Buff Stadium to see their native son pitch. Thus was born the nickname for "Vinegar Bend" Mizell—a pitcher who two years later broke into the Cardinals starting lineup and eventually became an All-Star and later a U.S. Congressman.

Russell was never short of promotional stunt ideas with the Houston Buffs. On several occasions he talked players into getting married at home plate before a game.

Once, irritated with an umpire's previous game calling, he conspired for revenge in front of a full stadium the next time the ump was scheduled to call home plate. Knowing the umpire had an almost irrational fear of snakes, Buffs manager Al Hollingsworth had a rubber snake attached to a long, thin string buried near home plate. Then, during the game when the umpire bent over to sweep the plate off between innings, he had the Buffs ball boy yank the string and pull the snake in front of the umpire to the delight of several thousand fans.

Russell also had a motivational idea to encourage the Buffs power hitters to swing for the outer fences. Each time a Buff would hit a home run, that player would be awarded a case of Wheaties breakfast cereal at home plate prior to the next home game. The players, however, quickly got tired of eating all that cereal and started storing the cases of Wheaties beneath the stadium, which attracted rats and forced abandonment of the "Wheaties for Homers" program.

Buff Stadium had a centerfield barrier that measured a healthy 415 feet, but to keep the game exciting, the Buffs management delineated it with a rope to encourage easy game-enhancing ground-rule doubles. Although the stadium was designed for 12,000 fans, it was not unusual for the Buffs to have overflow crowds that were seated behind the centerfield rope.

In high-quality baseball ranging from Texas League playoff games to St. Louis Cardinal exhibition games, a number of future Hall of Fame players thrilled those diehard Houston baseball fans at Buff Stadium for thirty-four years. At one time or another names like Dizzy Dean, Solly Hemus, Joe Medwick, Pepper Martin, and Ken Boyer appeared on rosters at the games. And, of course, Vinegar Bend Mizell. Near the end of his life, an emaciated Babe Ruth visited the stadium to be honored.

There was never a lack of excitement at the games. Fights on the field were commonplace then—it was the period before today's prima donna players. Houston's first home-televised baseball game was broadcast from Buff Stadium, and during the game a fan approached the camera, placed a gun to his head, and committed suicide.

For thirty-four years Buff Stadium provided Houston with sport and entertainment probably unmatched by today's professional baseball.

But the summer of 1935 belonged to the Huntsville Prison Tigers.

1   "Prisoners to meet Oilers Here Today," *Houston Chronicle*, September 8, 1935, pg. 16.
2   "Prison Tigers Play Brenham Here Today," *Houston Post*, September 8, 1935, pg. 18.
3   "Brenham Wins Over Prison," *Houston Post*, August 18, 1935, pg. 8.
4   "Prison Tigers Whallop Lufkin," *Houston Post*, August 22, 1935, pg. 8.
5   "Brenham Wins Houston Post Tournament Title," *Houston Post*, September 3, 1935, pg. 11.
6   "Brenham Oilers Will Play Prison Tigers Sunday," *Houston Post*, September 4, 1935, pg. 11.
7   "Prison Nine to be Made Trusties for Jaunt to Buffalo Stadium Sunday," *Houston Chronicle*, September 5, 1935, pg. 18.
8   Ibid.
9   Simmons, *Assignment Huntsville*, pg. 88.

Chapter Eight

"Escape From Peckerwood Hill"— Chief Satanta

Just outside the city, in a manicured field, rows upon rows of small white crosses are symmetrically arranged—concrete and granite crosses silently standing at attention.

This field of nondescript concrete crosses, located north of Huntsville, Texas, is Captain Joe Byrd Cemetery—operated by the prison system for the burial of indigent and unclaimed inmates who die in prison. (photo by Gary Brown)

The cemetery is not Arlington and the city is not Washington, D.C. Far from that hallowed and sacred ground to the northeast, this cemetery is called Peckerwood Hill and is located on the northeast edge of Huntsville, Texas. The deceased here are not revered heroes but, instead, the unnamed or unclaimed.

Officially known as Captain Joe Byrd Cemetery but referred to historically as Peckerwood Hill, this twenty-two-acre cemetery is the resting place for over 1,700 indigent convicts who were unclaimed or unwanted at the time of their death.

If the deceased inmate's family cannot be located or cannot afford to pay for a private burial, the plot is free and the state assumes responsibility. One source claims that one in three inmates who die in Texas prisons today is buried at Peckerwood Hill.

Almost a century after his death, this simple stone is the only legacy of a Texas criminal who died unclaimed and unwanted. Even his full name is unknown. (photo by Gary Brown)

Inmates are assigned a plot and given a pauper's funeral, with a short and simple Christian graveside ceremony unless the inmate has previously requested a final service in some other religious faith. Digging of the gravesite, burial, and cemetery care are all done by other inmates.

There is an aura of sadness here not softened by the often horrendous pasts of these unwanted corpses. Institutional imprisonment by its very nature tears at any shreds of self-respect of the living, but burial in Peckerwood Hill somehow seems the final insult the world can bestow on its outcasts.

The dates on the markers in the background are grim reminders that even today "Peckerwood Hill" provides the final resting place for indigent inmates in Texas. Concrete molds in the foreground represent a century-old method of making the simple grave markers. (photo by Gary Brown)

This inmate was the 182nd to be executed in the Texas electric chair (photo by Gary Brown)

While criminologists and social scientists debate the dehumanizing aspect of imprisonment on the living, the nameless crosses—most marked only by date of death and Texas prison numbers—finally and totally dehumanize the dead. Not only were they unwanted and unclaimed by their families, even the state ignores their individual names and assigns their final resting places with cold, emotionless numbers.

Actually there are some very valid reasons for this. Long before the cemetery was donated to the state in 1885, prisoners had been brought to the location and buried and then forgotten. Makeshift wooden crosses weathered and rotted away, and with the disintegrating wood went the names of those buried below the ground. Then the underbrush took over and reclaimed the land.

Peckerwood Hill would probably still be hidden beneath thick brush and thicket or even buried under an asphalt parking lot today had it not been for the efforts of prison captain Joe Byrd in the early 1900s. Using inmates from the nearby Walls Unit, Captain Byrd cleared the twenty-two-acre lot and reclaimed at least some of the permanent markers that were found there.

One of the earliest remaining markers is a headstone cut from inmate-quarried granite and dated 1870. During World War I a flu epidemic killed scores of convicts, and to control the outbreak, the bodies were quickly buried. The burials were so many and so often that many of the graves were simply listed by prison number or, in some cases, covered without identifying the bodies. At least four female convicts died during that epidemic and were buried at Peckerwood Hill.

This marker reminds us that not all criminals in the Joe Byrd Cemetery were male offenders. Very few women, however, were unclaimed at death and interred here over the years. (photo by Gary Brown)

These facts, and the belief that the land had served as a burial site for deceased slaves around Huntsville prior to the prison burials, mean nobody today knows for sure how many bodies are buried here. Of the over 1,700 known prisoner burials, more than two hundred died at the hands of the executioner. Many were hanged, others electrocuted in Old Sparky, and more recently killed by lethal injection. All but a dozen of the first one hundred men electrocuted in the electric chair are buried here. Other inmates died of old age while serving "life" sentences, some were killed by other inmates, and a few were killed while trying to escape.

The policy of anonymity is not absolute at Peckerwood Hill. Some markers do contain names, but most do not. Many, if not most, recent burials remain nameless—often at the request of the inmate's family, who do not want the family name associated forever with the Texas prison system. Some markers have been damaged or destroyed by vengeful members of a victim's family, and some stones of infamous or notorious convicts have been stolen or defaced.

One burial site is marked by an unusually large white stone, about three feet tall, inscribed:

Lee Smith
97036
At Rest
In Memory of
Rodeo Pals
October
26—1941

"Lee was a convict cowboy, a real good man with horses and cattle, but a mean man," Joe Byrd once told the *Houston Chronicle*. "He was trying to take another prisoner's commissary when a third convict bashed his skull in before I could get to them. The other cowboys chipped in and bought that big stone."[1]

Lee Smith was killed trying to "hog" another inmate for commissary. He is buried today at Joe Byrd Cemetery. (photo by Gary Brown)

After burial, the state does not re-cover the plot with sod, so it is up to nature to reclaim the bare earth above the body. It is almost as if Mother Earth alone is willing to accept and claim these indigent convicts when humans refuse.

Smith's marker stands out among the rows of over 1,700 smaller white crosses, but another gravesite is the focal point of Peckerwood Hill. Located in the shade beneath a large tree near the center of the cemetery, another large stone is surrounded by a low fence of three-inch pipe painted silver. But the size and location of this marker are not all that make it unusual in this uniform, anonymous, and institutionalized cemetery: This grave is also empty. It is the former burial site of Chief Satanta—famous (or infamous) Kiowa chief during the bloody Plains wars in Texas.

Like so many other notorious figures who served time in Texas prisons, Chief Satanta was controversial. To this day

Kiowa Chief Satanta died as a prisoner in the Texas prison system in 1878 and was buried for 85 years at "Peckerwood Hill" until his ancestors arranged to transfer his remains to Fort Sill, Oklahoma. (photo by Gary Brown)

historians debate his role in the bloody Indian conflicts of the latter 1800s. Known historically to the Kiowa as *Set'tainte*, or "White Bear," Chief Satanta is remembered reverently as a leader who "fought a long, hard battle for his people to keep the land they loved to hunt and live on." To Texas prison officials in the 1870s, he was known as Inmate Number 2107.

His earthly life ended inside the Huntsville Walls Unit on October 11, 1878, and he was buried beneath a shade tree in Peckerwood Hill. But his story did not end with his pauper's interrment. His remains and his "spirit" achieved what so many other prisoners have longed for and failed to achieve: Chief Satanta in the end escaped Peckerwood Hill and the Texas prison system.

Satanta was born sometime around 1820 in what is today either Kansas or Oklahoma. In the early 1800s the Plains

Indians—especially the Kiowa—ruled their territory almost unchallenged. As Satanta grew into young adulthood, the power of the Kiowa was steadily reduced to that of reservation life. As a teenager and young man he is believed to have been a warrior in the continuous wars between the Plains tribes, and it is believed that his first forays into Texas were before the 1850s.

By the end of the U.S. Civil War, he had risen in rank within the Kiowa Nation. In the post-war wave of white immigration to the West, Satanta and other Kiowa chiefs began a campaign of raids that took him at one point into the Panhandle of Texas where his raiding party killed a settler and kidnapped the man's wife and children.

In 1867 he was a Kiowa co-signatory of the Medicine Lodge Treaty created to establish an end to the fighting between Native Americans and white settlers while establishing reservations for the Kiowa and other tribes.

Within a year, however, he and the other Kiowa leaders had become frustrated with the unfulfilled treaty provisions and with reservation life and were once again involved in running battles with white settlers and the U.S. Army.

By 1871 white settlers in Texas were complaining of Native American raiding parties crossing the Red River into Texas territory and striking settlements. On May 15 over a hundred Kiowas, Comanches, Kiowa-Apaches, Arapahos, and Cheyenne from the Fort Sill Reservation crossed the Red River into Texas and three days later attacked a wagon train belonging to a freighting contractor named Henry Warren, traveling on the Butterfield Overland Mail route. They killed the wagon master and six teamsters, but in the battle, five teamsters managed to escape.

Incredibly, Chief Satanta and the other leaders led their war party back to Fort Sill to claim rations and announced to

Satanta, chief of the Kiowa, was imprisoned in the Texas prison system and died at Huntsville in 1878. (photo courtesy of Western History Collections, University of Oklahoma Library, Soule)

the agent there that they had participated in what was already becoming known as the Warren Wagon Train Raid.

Chief Satanta and another Kiowa leader named Big Tree were arrested at Fort Sill and returned to Jacksboro, Texas, where they were tried by a Texas jury and convicted of seven counts of murder in the Warren massacre.

Both leaders were sentenced to death by hanging, but Texas Governor Edmund Davis, no doubt in part fearing Kiowa and other Native American retaliation against settlers in unprotected areas of Texas, commuted their sentences to life imprisonment. November 2, 1871, Satanta and Big Tree were processed into the state penitentiary at Huntsville as inmates.

It was Chief Satanta's first, but not last, visit to Huntsville as a convicted felon. His prison records show he was "Set at Liberty" by Governor Davis on August 19, 1873. After twenty-three months the governor agreed to parole Satanta and Big Tree as a show of "good faith" in an attempt to stem further frontier violence. It was a ploy that failed miserably, however, when the various Native American tribes elected to enter the Red River War of 1874.

Despite publicly opposing Kiowa entrance into the conflict, Satanta was later identified as involved in the war—a violation of his parole—and rearrested and returned to Huntsville on September 17, 1874, serving a life sentence. The handwritten entry in his prison record indicates Lieutenant General Sheridan returned him as a parole violator.

For four years Chief Satanta did time at Huntsville. During that period several important public Texans advocated his release, including the superintendent of the penitentiary, Thomas J. Goree. Federal government officials and U.S. Army officers, however, campaigned to keep him in prison, and on October 11, 1878, it is alleged that he slashed his wrists. As he was being taken to the second floor of the prison hospital, he jumped off the landing and killed himself.

Chief Satanta was a controversial figure all of his adult life. To his people he was a revered leader; to white settlers he was a cold-blooded killer. To politicians he was a pawn in efforts to placate and pacify the Kiowa Nation. To Texas prison officials he was an aging prisoner who no longer constituted a threat to society. In death the controversy continued.

The old handwritten record of his arrival at Huntsville is maintained today in the Archives Division of the Texas State Library in Austin. In the comment section of his entry is the statement "Died fr. Effects of fall rec'd by voluntarily jumping from Hospital landing (2d story) Oct 11th 1878."[2] The official prison version of his death, therefore, was suicide.

But many Kiowa believed he was killed—pushed from the second floor landing. Yet others have seen his suicide—if it was in fact a suicide—as an act of warrior defiance in denying the prison system the ability to imprison him. They had his body, but not his spirit.

Texas did, in fact, have his body. Chief Satanta was interred in Peckerwood Hill in 1878, and Kiowa leaders immediately began a campaign to have his remains returned to Oklahoma where he could be interred with other Kiowa warriors and leaders at Fort Sill.

For eighty-five years Chief Satanta remained buried at Peckerwood Hill until the fifty-eighth Texas Legislature passed a bill allowing his grandson to remove his remains to Oklahoma.

In June 1963 his grandson, James Auchiah, and other Kiowa leaders performed a ceremony known as "smoking the grave" in Peckerwood Hill. Building a small fire at the foot of his grave, the Kiowa sprinkled dust from Fort Sill and cedar shavings into the flames to promote the transporting of Chief Satanta's spirit through the smoke.

Texas inmates then dug up the remains of the Kiowa leader: a few bones and one tooth. When those meager remains were reburied at Fort Sill, over two thousand Kiowas celebrated the final reinterrment of Chief Satanta.

Today Captain Joe Byrd Cemetery continues to provide the final resting place for the indigent, the unwanted, and the unclaimed. But so far as is known, Kiowa Chief Satanta— Inmate Number 2107—is the only prisoner to escape Peckerwood Hill.

1   *Houston Chronicle*, July 7, 1963 (from the vertical files at the Eugene C. Barker Texas History Collections, University of Texas at Austin).
2   Texas State Library and Archives, Call No. 1998/038-149, pg. 106, line 7.

Chapter Nine

"The Meanest Man in Texas"— Clyde Thompson

During a quarter-century spent in the Texas prison system, Clyde Thompson picked up a number of nicknames: "Meanest man in Texas," "Man without a soul," "Born killer but a coward at heart," "Kick killer," and "Thrill killer" are just a few.

Descriptions of his character and attitude weren't any better: "Will slay a fellow man for the love of the kill," "Thinks no more of killing a person than a normal person does of lighting a cigar," and "Kills just to see him [the victim] kick" were just some of the media and prison characterizations of Clyde Thompson.

But of all these derogatory descriptions, the suggestion that he was the "Meanest man in Texas" had to have been the harshest. It was the Texas Department of Corrections general manager who made that charge, and he did so over a radio program broadcast statewide.

Clyde Thompson spent nearly three decades in prison—much of it in solitary confinement—but his worst period was during the 1930s. How could this man—incarcerated in the same prison system as violent criminals like Clyde Barrow, Roy Thornton, Joe Palmer, Raymond Hamilton, and Charlie Frazier—be dubbed the meanest man in Texas?

He did it the old-fashioned way; he earned it.

Clyde Thompson entered the Texas prison system in March of 1931 with two murder convictions at the age of nineteen and the youngest convict to ever be assigned to the death cells at that time. He was assigned an inmate number, EX-83, and given an execution date of sixty days. "EX-83" indicated he was scheduled to be the eighty-third Texas convict executed in the electric chair.

Born in 1911, he was the illiterate son of a Bible salesman and part-time preacher when, at the age of seventeen, he confessed to the killing of two men in north central Eastland County, Texas. The trial had received wide coverage because of his age and because of accusations that he claimed to have killed "just to see him kick"—a charge he always denied.

He had been sentenced to death, and while awaiting an appeal he gained further notoriety when he was charged with instigating a riot in the Dallas County Jail in May of 1930 and then exposing his bare buttocks to reporters and photographers. A pattern of resistance to all authority, especially correctional, and the development of an extreme level of personal rage began to build up and boil over from inside him.

His appeal was denied, and in March 1931 he arrived at the Huntsville Walls Unit and was assigned to the death cells. There, he raged and fumed about the disparity between his death sentence and the relatively light punishment a co-defendant had received. When his ranting and screaming failed to obtain a stay of execution, he began feigning insanity—refusing to wash, shave, have his hair cut, or talk with anybody in an intelligible manner.

On the day of his scheduled execution, an inmate barber was brought to his cell and areas on his left leg and on his head were shaved in preparation for the electrodes being taped on as he was positioned in Old Sparky, Texas's electric chair.

Then, on this same day, the warden notified him only seven hours before he was to die that Governor Ross Sterling had commuted his death sentence to a life term. Perhaps his extended period at "acting" crazy had finally become a reality to him, or maybe he was just so full of hatred. Whatever the case, he fought guards trying to remove him from his death cell, claiming the state was just trying to trick him to get him into the electric chair.

After a couple of months assigned to the "crazy row" for prisoners with emotional or mental problems, he was released into the general inmate population. Almost immediately he and his cellmate began tunneling out of the Walls Unit from a sewer line within the prison compound. During this period he is thought to have met Clyde Barrow at least briefly while Barrow was being treated for the two toes he had had cut off to get off the Eastham prison farm.

Between his terrible behavior in the death cells and this escape attempt, prison officials had had enough. Thompson was shackled, loaded onto "Uncle Bud" Russell's chain bus, and transported to the hard-core prison farm unit south of Houston called the Retrieve Unit.

He continued to be a disciplinary nightmare for prison officials. On January 19, 1933, he participated in a break from a work gang, but an inmate "snitch" named Tommy Reis gave them away, and he was quickly caught by mounted guards. The guards shot two other escaping inmates; one died in the field.

After a particularly brutal stint in solitary confinement at Retrieve, he was once again released back into general population and assigned to a work squad. There, he rejoined inmate Barney Allen (who had been shot but survived during the escape attempt), and a confrontation occurred between the two and Tommy Reis, who had alerted guards that they were escaping in the field.

When the confrontation ended, Reis was dead and Thompson was accused of repeatedly stabbing the "snitch" while Allen had held him from behind.

Thompson and Allen were transferred to the Brazoria County Jail in nearby Angleton, and trials were scheduled early in March 1933. Clyde Thompson had only been in prison two years, but he had already gained statewide notoriety with what was obviously a media penchant to emphasize his bad characteristics.

"Clyde Thompson, apparently, is unaffected by the trial," the *Angleton Times* reported on March 3. "This is the third time he has been on trial for his life. He entered the Court room smiling and at no time during the day did he appear worried."[1]

A parade of Retrieve inmate witnesses took the stand, and the prosecutor entered into evidence the bloody "shank" that Thompson had used to kill Reis. The jury was selected and seated by noon, the arguments finished by 5:30 that afternoon, and the jury returned a verdict of guilty. Clyde Thompson escaped the death sentence one more time but in the process picked up his second life sentence. It had been a close call; the jury had voted 11 to 1 in favor of death. One stubborn juror had kept him from receiving another death sentence.

During his trial, his father, stepmother, and sisters were in attendance at the Angleton courtroom. As had been the case in his first trials for the murder of the two brothers in Eastland County, his father had remained by his side, supporting him and providing the best possible legal council he could on his limited income. In a world that Clyde Thompson had come to hate and despise, it was almost always his father to whom he could turn for support during the many troubles he found himself in. He was probably the only person in the world to whom Clyde Thompson could relate.

Clyde was returned to Retrieve and his work squad, and during that summer it is thought he came into contact with Roy Thornton, who was the husband of Bonnie Parker. At that time Bonnie was already making headlines as Clyde Barrow's criminal partner.

It was also during this period that, for an infraction of the rules, Clyde Thompson was held down on the floor and given twenty-two lashes with the infamous "bat"—a leather strap designed to inflict maximum pain and suffering on any inmate it was administered to.

During January 1935 his hopes for a prison release were buoyed by the news that Governor Miriam Ferguson had commuted his two life sentences to fifteen years as one of her final acts before leaving the governor's office.

Just when he thought he could see the possibility of freedom, he was notified by the Texas Attorney General's Office that only his initial life sentence was affected by the governor's ruling. That meant, in effect, he was now serving one life sentence plus fifteen years. Governor Ferguson's commutation did not, in reality, reduce his sentence one single day.

His attitude, already bad, hardened even more and so did his relations with guards and other inmates.

On May 29, 1935, he was involved in another fight with an inmate, and again the other convict ended up dead—this time with five savage stab wounds in his chest. Thompson later claimed the other inmate was attempting to "turn him out" or force him to be a "girlfriend." In other words, he was claiming self-defense.

Two days later, May 31, the *Angleton Times* reported that "thrill killer" Clyde Thompson and two other convicts had been charged with murder after Everet Melvin had been found stabbed five times in the chest, at least one of the blows reaching his heart.

Information obtained at the inquest brought out the fact that Thompson, Hall, Ebers and Melvin were grouped by themselves, just after they had completed their evening meal. They began scuffling between their bunks and were ordered to separate. Clyde went one way and the victim another. Melvin walked a few paces and then fell dead.

Thompson was then ordered to "come out of there." He obeyed at once.

"Give me the knife!" Thompson was ordered, and it was stated that he immediately handed over a bloody, hand-made dirk.

After the killing, Thompson glumly remarked to Capt. I.K. Kelley, farm manager, that he was "in trouble again" when the captain rushed to the barracks following the stabbing.

"Well, Cap," drawled Thompson, "it looks like I'm in trouble again."[2]

The *Times* article concluded that Thompson had killed three times before. Again the "thrill killer" and "kick killer" tags were applied to Clyde Thompson: "In the killing of two Eastland County brothers, he told officers, 'I killed them just to see them kick.'"

Thompson was first transferred to Huntsville during his arraignment and then back to the Brazoria County Jail where he stood trial for murder the second time in just over two years.

His viciousness, brutality, and hatred for criminal justice authorities and other inmates had by this time become the focal point of the charges against him in his murder of Everet Melvin. For a combination of factors, his own personal safety as well as those assigned to detain and guard him, Texas

Rangers were posted to observe his cell around the clock while he was held in the Brazoria County Jail.

For a second time his father traveled to Angleton to sit in the same courtroom and watch as Clyde was tried for murder with the possibility that he could be sentenced to death.

Thompson's attorneys, who included Frank Judkins of Eastland, were considered to be extremely capable. Ironically, Judkins had been the county attorney in Eastland County who had successfully prosecuted Clyde Thompson for the first two murder charges and obtained Thompson's original death sentence only to later spearhead the efforts to obtain his commutation to life.

Again, the prosecution called to the stand a parade of inmate witnesses who testified that Ed Ebers had held Melvin from behind while Clyde Thompson stabbed him. Those same inmates also testified that they felt Thompson was completely sane when he did the killing. To Thompson, this was only one more case of betrayal of the "inmate code" by the very convicts he would eventually be released back to.

That Thompson had used the knife to kill Melvin was never in question. On the advice of Judkins, he had based his plea on the grounds of insanity. As his father sat behind him in the courtroom, Clyde Thompson listened as his aunt, brother, and other relatives took the stand to plead for his life on the grounds he was not sane at the time of the killing.

Then Judkins changed tactics and assumed the position that Thompson had acted in self-defense. Now, Clyde Thompson took the stand and testified in his own defense. As the cross-examination began to delve into the specifics of Thompson's accusations that Melvin was coercing him for sex, the judge ordered all women out of the courtroom until the questioning was finished.

The case went to the jury, and at 10:00 P.M. on Thursday, July 25, 1935, the jury returned a verdict. The *Angleton Times*

This July 1935 banner headline refers to an inmate murder at the Retrieve Unit involving the infamous Clyde Thompson. A sub-headline also refers to Thompson's reputation as a "thrill killer." Years later Thompson would be labeled the "Meanest man in Texas" and be welded into an abandoned morgue building to segregate him from staff and other inmates.

reported "Clyde and his relatives, who have remained with him throughout the trial, were present when the verdict was read."

"Thompson came into the court with his head up, though decidedly pale," the *Times* reported. "He stood firmly and without visible fear. After he heard the verdict he broke down, crying with joy. His father and other members of his family also displayed emotion as it was learned the convict's life had been spared."[3]

Once again, Clyde Thompson had avoided the electric chair. But he had received his fourth murder conviction and his third life sentence. The newspaper sounded almost disappointed at the final verdict: "Thompson, the alleged 'thrill killer' from Eastland County, received just another life sentence which it is impossible for him to serve."

In the aftermath of the trial, the judge filed contempt of court charges on six Houston newsmen and reporters who had defied his gag order not to publish testimony during the Thompson trial since the trials of Ebers and Raymond Hall were still on the docket.

Ed Ebers, who had held Melvin from behind, later pled guilty and plea-bargained his way to a fifty-year sentence. Raymond Hall pled not guilty, and his defense attorney again called to the stand a number of Retrieve inmates who testified that Hall had been on his own bunk at the time of the killing. His trial ended in a hung jury, and he was eventually transferred to Huntsville for retrial.

But to Thompson, back at Retrieve, it was one more case of inmate betrayal. At times during his trial and that of Hall, it did appear the inmate testimony was geared at removing him from their midst by advocating the death sentence. Although the title "meanest man in Texas" had not been applied to him yet, Clyde Thompson had achieved the distinction of being violent and incorrigible—even to the hardened convicts at Retrieve.

Immediately after receiving his third life sentence, Thompson was transferred from Retrieve to the Walls Unit in Huntsville—arriving in mid-August 1935—just after the execution of Raymond Hamilton and Joe Palmer for their roles in the death cell escape earlier that year.

From Huntsville, the prison system sent this "hard-core" criminal to the Central Unit near Sugarland, Texas. Clyde Thompson was twenty-four years old when he climbed off Bud Russell's chain bus. He was also the killer of four men—two of them inmates inside prison—and perpetrator of escape attempts at the Walls Unit and at Retrieve.

It's not surprising that prison officials at Central kept him in solitary during most of his stay at that unit. Within a few months a new work camp for maximum-risk inmates was opened on the infamous Eastham Unit, and Thompson was transferred there early in 1936.

At Eastham he found himself incarcerated with other "hard-core" convicts whom the prison officials intended to keep under the highest level of security.

It was also at Eastham that he came into contact with the already legendary escape artist named Charlie Frazier. Frazier and Thompson were assigned to the same work squad, and two escape plans designed by Frazier were thwarted during that period. Then in October 1937 one of Frazier's plans was actually implemented, but Thompson and two other inmates, including Bonnie Parker's husband, Roy Thornton, were shot and wounded.

In the shootout, Thompson had obtained a pistol and exchanged fire with the guards before being wounded himself. Shot in the right arm, he spent several weeks in the prison hospital before being reassigned to his work squad. Once again, he learned, he and the others had been thwarted by another inmate "snitch."

By now he was almost totally unmanageable and avoided even by the other convicts, most of whom were considered by the prison system to be violent offenders themselves.

Within three weeks of the failed escape attempt, Thompson was charged with another murder of a fellow inmate. Records do not indicate if the victim was suspected of being the convict who had "snitched" the escape plan, but Thompson was once again placed in solitary confinement.

While he was there, prison officials sent a guard and building tenders to his cell to administer the "bat" once more to him. Aware that guards were instructed not to administer the beatings to a bleeding man, Thompson took a razor and intentionally sliced his buttocks in a manner that left no uncut area to be struck with the "bat."

Prison administrators, however, had had their fill with Thompson, his killings, and his escape attempts. The punishment was administered anyway, with Thompson screaming and threatening to kill everybody involved.[4]

This was the period of his life when the "Meanest man in Texas" title was applied to him by the prison director. The media, always ready to sensationalize any news relating to Thompson, quickly grabbed the term and splashed it over headlines across Texas.

His self-mutilation with the razor only intensified his reputation as an out-of-control, ultra-violent sociopath. Then, without explanation, the murder charges were dropped.

Thompson emerged from solitary only to discover that his father had died. In Texas prisons during the 1930s it was a common practice for prison officials to allow inmates—even some death cell convicts—furloughs to attend the funerals of parents. In Thompson's case, however, prison authorities did not even notify him of the death of his father until after the funeral had been conducted.

Thompson at this time had the reputation among guards and inmates of being a crazy man who could relate to no other human being. His father, however, had remained by his side all his life: from the Eastland County trials to the two murder trials in Brazoria County. That prison officials would deny him a furlough—or even inform him of his father's death—sent him even further into the throes of self-destruction and hatred against the system that was imprisoning him.

Threatening to kill everyone around him—including himself—he was transferred from the Eastham Unit back to Huntsville. There, even the death cells were not considered secure enough to hold him—Joe Palmer and Raymond Hamilton after all had escaped those very cells in 1935. The old morgue was activated, marble slabs were removed, and a heavy gauge welded steel door was installed.

There, in almost complete darkness and isolation, the Texas prison system found a secure place to imprison Clyde Thompson to protect themselves and other inmates from him.

The "Meanest man in Texas" had bottomed out.

As he ranted, raved, and threatened from inside his morgue-cell, guards generally avoided him except to deliver his meals and have a building tender exchange the bucket containing water.

But one guard ventured a suggestion: Thompson needed something to read. Thompson agreed, and the warden approved him having a Bible in the cell. A small window was cut into the door so he had at least limited light during the daytime hours.

Thompson, who was nearly illiterate, struggled with the wording of the Bible. Over time his behavior improved, and he was allowed a radio that he used to listen to Sunday sermon broadcasts and learn to pronounce biblical words.

His good behavior continued, and he was released from his morgue-cell after five years. It was 1944 and he was thirty-three years old.

With three escape attempts on his record, he was transferred from the morgue to the death cells for security reasons. There he became involved in religious activities and baptized a number of death cell convicts. He was eventually released from the maximum-security death cells into the general population and became a chaplain's assistant.

Then in the spring of 1946 he was transferred to the Wynne Farm on the outskirts of Huntsville, and in March of 1951 he returned to Brazoria County when he was sent to the Ramsey Farm.

Then in March 1951 his change in behavior and attitude and his work with the religious programs on the various units paid off when he received a conditional pardon and release from prison.

The "Meanest man in Texas" had worked himself out of the hellhole in that abandoned prison morgue to the freedom of Texas parole. It had taken a quarter-century of his life, and behind him remained four murder convictions, two unarmed escape attempts, and one shootout attempt.

Like so many convicts who finally find themselves bottomed out with nowhere to go but up, Clyde Thompson in the end turned to religion. It is not an unusual phenomenon in prison; even the infamous Charlie Frazier died a religious convert while a prisoner in a Louisiana hospital, and feared gunfighter John Wesley Hardin had taught Sunday school at the Huntsville Unit.

But many of these religious "conversions" do not last once the inmate gets what he wants. In Clyde Thompson's case, however, his religion sustained him the remainder of his life outside prison.

Immediately after parole he became involved in prison religious programs in Lubbock, Huntsville, and other prison and jail locations around Texas. Until his death, he traveled widely across the state, working with inmates and youth at risk.

In 1963 he was unconditionally pardoned by Texas Governor John Connally and eventually became an ordained minister. On July 2, 1979, Clyde died as a result of cardiac arrest.

Yes, during a quarter-century in the Texas prison system, Clyde Thompson picked up a number of nicknames: "Meanest man in Texas," "Man without a soul," "Born killer but a coward at heart," "Kick killer," and "Thrill killer."

At the end of his life, he had picked up one more: "Reverend Thompson." And yes, he picked them all up the old-fashioned way; he earned them.

This 1930s Texas prison photograph shows the conditions often endured by inmates such as Clyde Barrow, Joe Palmer, Raymond Hamilton, Charlie Frazier, and Clyde Thompson. (photo source: Texas State Archives, courtesy of Jester III Unit, Texas Department of Criminal Justice).

1   *Angleton Times*, March 3, 1933, front page.
2   *Angleton Times*, May 31, 1935, front page.
3   *Angleton Times*, July 26, 1935, front page.

Chapter Ten

"Texas's Fastest and Wildest Rodeo Cowboy"— O'Neal Browning

In 1931 Texas, baseball reigned king among sports activities. Semi-pro and minor league teams all over Texas dominated the sports pages throughout the summer, and speculation about spring rosters filled the winter month columns.

There was one other sport that might—just might—have rivaled baseball for popularity in Texas in the 1930s. Almost every small town and virtually every large city had a rodeo arena where local cowboys competed for bull and steer riding honors. Occasionally they might pick up a little money, but usually the winner was lucky to get a plated belt buckle. For the most part, the sport of rodeo was done for the pure love of the competition—against both man and beast.

For the Texas prison system in 1930, recreation had been limited mostly to crude baseball fields on the units in which convicts were allowed to play each other on Sunday afternoons. In fact, it was on the Huntsville Walls Unit baseball field that the first Texas Prison Rodeo was staged.

This is why the Texas Prison Rodeo was billed the "Wildest Show on Earth." (photo courtesy of Texas State Archives)

That first rodeo, held in 1931, was designed as a recreational outlet for inmates and to give some entertainment for prison guards and their families. Initially the rodeo was not envisioned as an entertainment venue for the general public.

The schedule was set for every Sunday afternoon during October, and the Texas Prison Rodeo never varied from that program except for 1943 when the events of World War II and the massive mobilization of men in the military led to cancellation.

Not only did the prison system provide the cowboys for the rodeo, but all livestock was selected from the vast herds located on the various farm units around the state.

Prison director and the moving force behind the creation of the rodeo, Lee Simmons, named the original rodeo "Texas' Fastest and Wildest Rodeo." In later years prison officials

The Texas Prison Rodeo featured inmate cowboys and prison-raised livestock. The annual event became a Texas cultural highlight before it was discontinued in the 1980s. (photo courtesy of Texas State Archives)

changed the name to the "World's Fastest and Wildest Rodeo" and finally "The Wildest Show on Earth."

Although designed as a private affair for inmates and prison staff, the public soon appeared at the Sunday performances that very first year. Within two years public attendance swelled from a handful of outsiders to almost 15,000, prompting prison officials to erect wooden stands and begin charging admission.

In the early years, prison officials tried to limit competition to inmates with ranch or rodeo experience but soon opened the rodeos to convicts with clean records for the year preceding the annual event. With time and success of the rodeo, inmate participation was increased when forty "Red Shirt"

This convict cowboy may have been a car thief or a murderer on the outside. The horse obviously doesn't care and wasn't impressed. (photo courtesy of Texas State Archives)

cowboys were added to perform as a special daredevil squad entertaining the public by doing nontraditional rodeo chores such as milking wild cows. Other inmates would be chosen to work as clowns and general arena maintenance workers.

Two try-out Sundays were held each September, and 100 convict cowboys were selected for the big show in October. For many inmates with long-term sentences, qualifying for the Texas Prison Rodeo was their only contact with the outside world and the public. For many of them, preparation for the rodeo became a yearlong training program with workouts in the gyms and a very powerful incentive to maintain a clean disciplinary record.

The fact that the Texas Prison Rodeo was conducted under the strict guidelines of prison security didn't detract from the authenticity of the events. In nearly every manner, the rodeo at Huntsville mirrored the famous rodeos held in Cheyenne, Houston, and Santa Fe.

Each Sunday inmate cowboys competed in calf roping, saddle and bareback bronc riding, bull riding, chute dogging, and wild horse races. Other events, such as bareback basketball and wild cow milking, were mostly for crowd entertainment. Some events were unique to prison rodeo. The "Hard Money" event involved tying a Bull Durham tobacco pouch filled with cash between the horns of a particularly mean bull. The forty "Red Shirts" would then compete to remove the pouch and claim the money. By the 1980s collections were circulating among the crowds to "up the ante," and prizes represented considerable money for the winning convict.

In the "Mad Scramble" ten tough bulls were saddled, mounted, and released at the same time—snorting and bucking as the inmates in the saddles tried to race them to the other side of the arena.

The only event missing from regular professional rodeo venues was the steer wrestling—eliminated from the program in 1933.

By 1950 the crowds had become so large that fans were being turned away, and in 1950 a concrete and steel rodeo stadium was constructed. Except for the 1943 war-related cancellation, the only rodeo that wasn't held in Huntsville was the 1950 event that was held in Dallas while the new stadium was being constructed.

Half-time entertainment was provided by inmate choirs and bands and often proved as entertaining and popular as the rodeo events themselves. When the new stadium opened in the 1950s, "big name" rodeo entertainers staged exhibitions while Hollywood and show business singers became major drawing cards. By the 1980s the Texas Prison Rodeo was matching the world-class Houston Livestock Show and Rodeo in terms of providing professional country and western musical entertainment.

In 1972 competition events for inmate women were included in the rodeo programs: greased pig sacking, calf scramble, calf roping, and barrel racing were popular events, but many visitors complained that some of the events were blatantly designed to be humiliating for the women convicts participating. In 1981 the women's prison unit was moved from Huntsville, and female inmate participation in the Texas Prison Rodeo ended.

The prison rodeo was truly "Texas' Fastest and Wildest Rodeo." Injuries were common due to the "let 'er rip" attitude of the convict cowboys. From the first rodeo in 1931 until the final show in 1986 two inmate cowboys were killed in the arena.

O'Neal Browning was born the year prison director Lee Simmons began formulating the plans for the first Texas Prison Rodeo. For Browning, who would eventually become TDC Inmate #113284, handling livestock and farm animals was something he learned early in life. Raised on a family farm, at age sixteen he got a job in 1946 feeding stock at the Houston Fat Stock Show and Rodeo (now the Houston Livestock Show and Rodeo). While working there, he watched the would-be cowboys hanging around the chutes waiting to work the broncs and bulls prior to the opening of the annual event.

"They were paying fellas five dollars a head to ride the bulls, so I watched for a while to see how they got down on the animal, how they held the rigging and all, and then I went over and said I wanted to ride a few. I was scared to death, but five dollars a head sounded like a fortune to me," Browning reported in 1974.[1]

He earned $100 that day and was hooked on rodeo competition for the rest of his life. Soon he was traveling around the Houston area to compete in the small-town rodeos that were popular in rural Texas immediately after World War II.

His mother objected to his rodeo riding on the grounds he could get hurt, but he continued competing anyway. In a high-risk sport where serious injuries are always a possibility, he lost a thumb while roping steers, but the "rodeo fever" still had a hold on him.

More serious objections came from his father, who whipped him regularly when he returned from the nearby competitions. To his father, O'Neal Browning's time was better spent working on the family farm than riding broncs or bulls in rodeos. In later years Browning admitted he was also drinking heavily during that period.

Still, he was riding, learning, and even earning small purses at the small-town rodeos.

It all came to a halt the night he stumbled home drunk and passed out in the house. Next morning the police woke him and charged him with the axe murder of his father. He pled guilty.

He processed into the prison system in the spring of 1949, and by October of the following year he was approved by prison authorities to compete in the annual Texas Prison Rodeo.

By 1950 the Texas Prison Rodeo had grown into a major sporting event in East Texas, and rules and traditions had been formalized. The most sought after award was the title of All-Around Cowboy, which went to the cowboy who won the most prize money over the period of the four-weekend rodeo. In addition to amassing the most prize money, an inmate cowboy also had to compete in at least one of the major riding events: bull, bareback, or saddle bronc.

In his first year at the rodeo, O'Neal Browning walked away with the engraved gold and silver belt buckle and title of All-Around Cowboy. Ironically, because of his age, he had to convince his mother to sign a release so he could participate.[2]

Saddle bronc riding was only one of four qualifying events to compete for the coveted "All-Around Cowboy" title. (photo courtesy of Texas State Archives)

But his success at the 1950 Texas Prison Rodeo did not erase the fact he was a young kid with a lifetime of prison time to serve. In 1951 he ran away from a cotton gin work crew, escaping, ironically, by horseback. Within days he was recaptured and returned to prison.

In 1954 he earned his second All-Around Cowboy championship and repeated again in 1956 and 1958. After serving nine years in prison, O'Neal Browning had established himself as the All-Around Cowboy with the most titles in the history of the prison rodeo. The record stands today, and his achievement of earning four individual titles during the decade of the 1950s was never matched in any following decade.

In 1962 he added to his personal record by earning his fifth All-Around Cowboy title. It was also the year he was first paroled from the Texas prison system. He returned, he claimed voluntarily, rather than work for the man he was paroled out to.

The following year he paroled again, and for the next two years he got to live the dream he had nurtured behind bars: He drove a cattle truck and broke horses for a living while competing in rodeos for purse money. He applied for and was granted membership in the Rodeo Cowboys Association making him—on a limited scale at least—a professional rodeo cowboy.

However his drinking got the better of him again, and he returned to prison in 1965 and immediately became involved with the Texas Prison Rodeo again. Sometime during that period he was sitting on the fence watching the bull riding event when another inmate cowboy was thrown from a bull then gored and mauled by the animal.

Browning jumped down from the fence and distracted the bull only to find himself backed up against the fencing and pinned between the bull's horns. "I've still got a couple of scars on both my sides," he reported in 1974. "I guess if I'd weighed a couple more pounds I'd be dead right now. Luckily, however, my waist just fit between the horns—except for an inch or so of hide which the bull managed to get when he pinned me."[3]

In 1968 he regained his title as All-Around Cowboy—the sixth time in his prison career.

Like all cowboys, however, age was catching up with him. At age thirty-nine he was injured again in 1969 when a bull named White Lightning threw him and broke some ribs and separated others. "It hurt to blink my eyes there for a few days," he recalled.[4]

The 1970 Texas Prison Rodeo got off to a bad beginning for Browning when in the first weekend, another bull broke his leg. It was a particularly bad accident and one all bull riders fear: The bull slipped and fell and stomped on Browning's leg as it got up.

For the remaining three Sundays, O'Neal Browning reported to the chutes on crutches and continued to ride towards the top purse and his seventh All-Around Cowboy title. It wasn't to happen that year but, in the process of competing with a badly broken leg, he finished sixth in the overall competition and added greatly to his already growing prison rodeo legend.

He never worked the rodeo out of his blood. Three years after the broken leg, at age forty-three, he captured his seventh All-Around Cowboy title. It was a record that would stand until the final weekend of October in 1986 when the Texas Prison Rodeo closed its gates for good.

The 1973 title came the hard way: bull riding, saddle bronc, bareback competition, and chute doggin'. That year Browning placed third in the bareback competition the first Sunday of October and followed the next week with firsts in saddle bronc and chute doggin'. On the fourth Sunday he placed second in saddle competition and in bull riding, which was enough to give him the overall championship for 1973. And all this at age forty-three!

His seven All-Around Cowboy titles and the fact he won them in each of three decades earned him celebrity status both among inmate cowboys and civilian rodeo visitors.

In 1974 he confided his intention to keep competing indefinitely and that he hoped to earn his eighth All-Around Cowboy title that year. He didn't; another inmate named George Huff won that year, and O'Neal Browning never again claimed the title.

His rodeo exploits did earn him one last honor, however, when the seventh annual "Sportsman of the Year" award was presented to him in 1973. The award was given annually for outstanding performance in whatever sport the recipient was playing, as well as for possessing those attributes that qualify him as a sportsman of the first order—leadership, fair play, and a competitive spirit.[5]

During the 1970s the annual attendance figures for the Texas Prison Rodeo often totaled 100,000 visitors. But during the latter years of the decade and the first years of the 1980s attendance began to dwindle.

In 1986, the final year of the event, the rodeo attendance was an estimated 50,000 fans and gate receipts totaled $450,000 before expenses were deducted. When engineers condemned the 1950 concrete and steel stadium and recommended a half-million dollars in renovations, the prison system was unable to maintain what had become a state tradition and East Texas annual cultural event.

From 1931 to 1986 the Texas Prison Rodeo showcased thousands of inmate cowboys, the best of professional country and western singers over the decades, and produced a host of convict cowboy legends that remain today within the brick and wire walls of the Texas prison units around the state.

Within the legions of inmate rodeo myth and fact, however, the name of O'Neal Browning remains the most famous, and his numerous personal rodeo records stand today as they did when he won seven All-Around Cowboy titles in the 1950s …and the 1960s…and the 1970s.

1   *Texas Parade*, Vol. 35, No. 5, October 1974, pg. 38.
2   "Browning: Seven Titles," *43rd Annual Texas Prison Rodeo*, Official Souvenir Program, Texas Department of Corrections, Huntsville, Texas, 1974, pg. 20.
3   Ibid., pg. 39.
4   Ibid.
5   Ibid., pg. 21.

(photo
courtesy of
Texas State
Archives)

(photo
courtesy of
Texas State
Archives)

Chapter Eleven

"No Man Can Arrest Me"—Gregorio Cortez

To most of us, translations from one language to another are at the worst an inconvenience: finding directions or ordering a meal. And to most of us, it is probably inconceivable that a translation could result in an eight-year stay in prison.

Yet such a linguistics problem contributed to the fact that Gregorio Cortez spent eight years in the Texas prison system. Even worse, that same simple translation error contributed to the deaths of at least nine people and the wounding of three others.

What is remarkable about Gregorio Cortez' trials, prison sentence, and appeals is not the story of his time at Huntsville —very little information is available about his eight years there. What is remarkable about his time with the Texas prison system is the story of how his arrest, trials, and imprisonment divided an already polarized Texas society.

And what was the root of this terrible mistake? It was the simple translation of the phrases "horse or mare," "want you or wanted," and "nothing or nobody."

To most Americans who don't work with livestock for a living, the word "horse" is a generic term for "mare," "gelding," "stallion," or even "pony." A horse can be male or female or young or old.

The Spanish language, however, is far more gender-specific. Spanish words are assigned gender in terms of masculine or feminine. To a Mexican or Spanish-speaking American, the Spanish word for horse is "*un caballo*" which is masculine. The expression "*una yegua*" also means horse, only in the feminine sense.

So while most English-speaking Americans use "horse" interchangeably to define male and female animals, most Spanish-speaking people differentiate by gender when using the term "horse" in everyday usage.

Not a problem for most of us today, but 1901 Texas was still a society based largely on horse culture. Horses were still the primary mode of transportation for most Texans, and the theft of a horse was a serious felony offense punishable by prison time—if the "really old" frontier code didn't take effect and the guilty party ended up dangling from a tree limb.

It was the theft of a horse early in 1901 that led to Gregorio Cortez' problems with the law—an event that would polarize Anglo and Mexican Texans for decades and send Cortez to prison for a third of his adult life.

Even today there are vast differences of opinion about him and facts have blurred into fable. To Mexican-American society in the early 1900s, Gregorio Cortez was a martyr; to Anglo-American Texans he was a murderous villain. Somewhere in between is probably the truth.

In June of 1901 the Karnes County sheriff, Brack Morris, received word from a nearby county that a "medium-sized Mexican with a big, red, broad-brimmed Mexican hat" had stolen a sorrel mare and that the horse had been tracked to Karnes County.

And so Sheriff Morris headed out into his South Texas county, looking for a Mexican horse thief who was "medium-sized." Asking around, he discovered that Andres Villarreal had recently purchased a sorrel mare. Morris talked with Villarreal and discovered that the horse had been sold by Gregorio Cortez.

While Karnes County had a high number of Mexican-heritage residents in 1901, it was still a relatively sparsely populated rural county, so the sheriff reasoned that Cortez— who was also "medium-sized"—could be considered a legitimate suspect.

Sheriff Morris decided to take a translator along when he went to question Cortez. To assist him, he picked one of his deputies, Boone Schoate, who claimed to speak "Mexican" pretty good. Morris and Schoate were accompanied by a third deputy, John Trimmel, when they went to Cortez' ranch on June 12.

From all indications, the trio of lawmen was simply going out to the Cortez home to ask some questions. They almost certainly weren't looking for trouble as evidenced by the fact that Shoate wasn't even armed and the three were traveling in a buggy—hardly the mode of transportation for confrontation or pursuit.

Before they arrived at Cortez' house, they stopped at a horse pen and Trimmel got out to look around. Sheriff Morris and Boone Schoate, the "translator," continued on to the house where they found Gregorio Cortez, his wife, Leonor, and his brother Romaldo on the front porch.

Upon seeing the approaching buggy, Gregorio had armed himself with a pistol, and as the two lawmen arrived, he sent Romaldo to meet them at the gate.

Morris, through Schoate, asked to speak to Gregorio himself. Schoate, it turned out, was not nearly the linguist he claimed to be. Clumsily he relayed the sheriff's request to Romaldo who relayed to the front porch: *Te quieren*," which is a common phrase for "they want to talk to you." Literally, however, it means "you are wanted," and Schoate took

Romaldo's statement to Gregorio to mean "they've come to get you"—suggesting to him, at least, an element of guilt.

Gregorio, hiding the pistol, got up from the porch and walked to the gate. Morris asked Gregorio if he had traded a horse to Andres Villarreal. Then the real problems began.

Schoate translated the question, using the term "*un caballo*" in the Anglo generic form. Cortez, hearing the Spanish word in the gender-specific meaning of "male horse," answered "no" since the horse he had traded Villarreal had been "*una yegua*" or a female horse. He had, in Spanish, told the truth.

Schoate, however, mistranslated the answer to mean that Cortez was denying making the translation and said so to Sheriff Morris. Morris, relying on Schoate's interpretation, decided Cortez was lying and announced he was going to arrest Gregorio.

Gregorio, still holding that his denial of trading a "male horse" was the truth, replied "*A mi no me arreste por nada*," or "you can't arrest me for nothing."

Schoate, who must have known by now he was in way over his head as a translator, again misunderstood. He told Sheriff Morris that Gregorio Cortez had replied "*A me no me arreste por nadie*," and translated it to mean "No white man can arrest me."

As Morris moved toward Gregorio, Romaldo interceded, and in the scuffle Romaldo was shot. In turn, Gregorio pulled his pistol and shot the sheriff. Schoate, who was unarmed, ran back toward the pens to get Trimmel. The two men then set out for the nearby town of Kenedy to get help.

In 1901 rural Texas was still often a lawless land, and the killing of a sheriff was serious business. At Kenedy, Trimmel and Schoate staggered into town and reported "an armed gang" of Mexican horse thieves. Within hours over 300 rangers, law officers, posses, militias, mobs, and private citizens were combing Karnes County for Gregorio Cortez.

After the shooting Cortez loaded his wounded brother, his wife, and four children into the buggy and sent them to the home of a friend. He then took out on foot, wearing regular shoes, and walked to Gonzales some eighty miles away where he visited a friend living on a ranch.

Gonzales County Sheriff Robert Glover suspected Cortez might head towards his county and learned where Gregorio was staying. In the resulting shootout, Glover and another man named Schnabel, who owned the land, were killed and Cortez escaped into the darkness.

From there he walked to the home of Ceferino Flores and borrowed a horse, which he literally rode to death near Stockdale.

By now it seemed every lawman in Texas had organized posses to pursue Cortez, and his flight to avoid arrest was starting to dominate state newspaper headlines.

Near Stockdale, in a field, he found a small brown mare that he saddled and mounted. That brown mare, a horse that was to become a legend in her own right, was the famous "yegua trigueña" that many later claimed was the best horse in Texas at the time.

Knowing the area he was in was crawling with posses and lynch mobs, he turned the mare southward for the Rio Grande.

For the next three days, Cortez and his yegua trigueña were pursued almost constantly for between 300 and 400 miles across the South Texas landscape.

Near Cotulla, the mare was injured and Cortez was forced to abandon her and continue on foot again. A train on the International-Great Northern Railroad route to Laredo was used to bring in new posses and fresh horses—the first time in

Texas that law officers had to do so to capture a fleeing suspect.

By now Cortez had a $1,000 reward—very sizeable in 1901—for his arrest. It was probably for the reward money that he was betrayed. Very near the banks of the Rio Grande and sanctuary in Mexico, Cortez was finally captured when Jesús González, one of his acquaintances, located him and led a posse to him on June 22, 1901, ten days after the encounter between Cortez and Sheriff Morris.

Those ten days of frantic escape from overwhelming odds had made him a Texas legend. To many Anglo-Texans, a vicious "sheriff-killer" was finally behind bars; but to many Mexican-Americans, Gregorio Cortez represented a legitimate and honorable affront to Anglo injustice towards Hispanics in Texas.

The resulting trials and eventual imprisonment became an emotional focal point for both factions.

Once he was captured, he was jailed in San Antonio, and a long legal fight began. The Miguel Hidalgo Workers' Society of San Antonio and other organizations collected funds. The fund raising became a "cause," uniting Texans of Mexican heritage throughout South Texas.

Through the massive newspaper coverage during his dash toward the Rio Grande, even a number of Anglo-Texans came to admire his cause and, given the often-contradictory facts of the Morris shooting, also contributed to his defense.

During the next three and a half years, Gregorio Cortez would be tried numerous times for the murders of Sheriff Brack Morris, Sheriff Robert Glover, and Henry Schnabel as well as for horse theft. He would be convicted of murder on all three counts only to have them all overturned on appeal. In time he would be acquitted of the murder charge involving Glover; acquitted of Morris' murder charge and retried on manslaughter charges; and never be retried for Schnabel's killing.

The first of his trials began in Gonzales on July 24, 1901. Eleven jurors found him guilty of the murder of Schnabel, but the lone holdout refused to convict and a compromise fifty-year sentence for second-degree murder was given. Cortez' attempt to appeal the case was denied. A mob of 300 men tried to lynch him.

Later that year he was tried in Pleasanton and sentenced to two years in prison for horse theft. He would also be tried and convicted in Karnes. During all these legal maneuverings, the press continued to headline his trials, and the Texas public that had become infatuated with his efforts to resist arrest now followed daily his attempts to resist conviction and imprisonment.

Then on January 15, 1902—possibly in part due to the publicity involved—the Texas Court of Criminal Appeals overturned the verdicts handed down in Gonzales, Pleasanton, and Karnes.

In Goliad he was tried for the murder of Sheriff Morris, but the trial ended in a hung jury. Later charges were filed against him in Wharton County, but the judge dismissed them for the lack of jurisdiction. At times it appeared the law enforcement officials were far more interested in convicting Cortez for the murder of two sheriffs and a deputy than were Texas juries and jurisdictional-oriented judges.

But his victories in the courtroom were not translating into personal freedom. Held without bond, he was transferred from court to court on the various murder and horse theft charges.

Then on March 12, 1903, his wife divorced him, alleging as part of her petition that Gregorio had physically and verbally abused her during the early years of their marriage and that she had remained with him only out of fear.

Sometime during this period he spent a year in the Harris County Jail where he almost died of pneumonia.

He would also be tried for Glover's murder in Columbus, and that jury convicted him not of murder, but of manslaughter, and sentenced Cortez to fifty years in prison.

His last trial was held April 25-30, 1904, at Corpus Christi. The jury found Cortez not guilty of murder in the death of Sheriff Morris—agreeing with Cortez' assertion of self-defense. The "not guilty" verdict, however, was a shallow victory for Gregorio Cortez since the Columbus manslaughter verdict had been upheld.

He entered the Huntsville Penitentiary on January 1, 1905. His prison sentence was remarkable not for any occurrences during his time served but for the events leading to his arrest and convictions prior to incarceration.

His transfer to Huntsville likewise drew prominent newspaper coverage. So well known had he become that the newspapers referred to him as "the famous Mexican."

> Gregorio Cortez, the famous Mexican, to whose hand is laid the killing of three officers—two sheriffs and one deputy—and one who has been sentenced to life imprisonment, spent last night in the Harris county jail. He was brought in by Captain Sisk, who will this morning take him to Huntsville where he will be consigned behind the walls, there to spend the remainder of this natural life, unless, perchance, the clemency of the State's chief executive is invoked in his behalf.[1]

The newspaper articles continued by reporting that Cortez "is well liked by the jail officers here. He never gave them any trouble and they treated him kindly. When he arrived last night he gave the hand of Night Keeper Trammell a hearty shake and evinced a gladness to see him." It was the kind of report prison officials wanted to see for new arrivals.

His official records at Huntsville recorded his height as five feet, nine inches, his weight as 144 pounds, his hair as black and wavy, his eyes as brown, and his complexion as "medium dark." In other words, he was a "medium-sized Mexican."

It appears that while he was in the various county jails for over three years, he had begun cutting other inmates' hair. When he was received at Huntsville he gave his occupation not as vaquero or farmer but as barber, and he seems to have been allowed to exercise that trade during his years in prison. His certificate of prison conduct reads, "Occupation, barber; habits, temperate; education, limited." In things other than books his education was wide.[2]

Efforts to obtain a pardon for him began as soon as he was processed into the state prison at Huntsville. The Board of Pardons Advisers eventually recommended a full pardon, and even Secretary of State F. C. Weinert worked to obtain one for him. Eventually the prison chaplain, the warden, and the chief clerk at Huntsville were among those writing the governor.[3] It would appear that the good rapport that Cortez had established with his county jailers carried over into his prison years at Huntsville.

Finally, in 1913, Texas had a governor, O.B. Colquitt, who was favorably disposed to pardon Cortez, and on July 14 the "famous Mexican" was issued a pardon. Emotions were still running high around the state, however, so Colquitt made the pardon "conditional."

Once released, Cortez thanked those who helped him recover his freedom—even visiting the governor in Austin to personally thank him. His imprisonment had been controversial from the time of his arrival at Huntsville. The *Houston Chronicle*, in reporting his release, acknowledged "There has always existed considerable doubt as to the killing of Sheriff Glover by Cortez.... It was never proven that Cortez was at the scene of the killing. In fact, a deputy sheriff declared afterward he thought Cortez was in Wilson County at the time."[4]

The *Austin Statesman*, in reporting his visit to Governor Colquitt, stated "The indeterminate sentence committee, while making a round of the penitentiaries, investigated the case of Cortez and reached the unanimous conclusion that he had been unjustly incarcerated."[5]

Shortly after his pardon and release, he went to Nuevo Laredo and fought with Victoriano Huerta in the Mexican Revolution. During the fighting he was wounded and returned to Manor, Texas, and later resettled at Anson. On February 28, 1916, he died at the age of forty-one in Anson; some reports state he had a heart attack, others that he succumbed to pneumonia.

Gregorio Cortez represents an unusual convict in the Texas prison system. His claims of innocence, which he never abandoned, had enough grounds for doubt that even the state officials in charge of incarcerating him campaigned for his release. Despite his death at a relatively young age, he had already become a legend in his own lifetime.

He remains one of the more famous prisoners to have served time in Texas prisons. Yet little is known of his incarceration years—his legendary status was achieved during his daring dash for freedom in Mexico on the also-legendary *yegua trigueña*.

To most of us, translations from one language to another are at worst an inconvenience. For Gregorio Cortez y Lira, however, the inconvenience cost him nearly a third of his life behind bars.

1   Trial coverage was often done on a "reporter-pool" basis, and identical stories appeared throughout Texas newspapers. An example would be the following coverage of his commitment to prison: "Gregorio Cortez To The Pen," *Brownsville Daily Herald*, January 4, 1905, front page; "Gregorio Cortez En Route To Pen," *San Antonio Express*, January 2, 1905, front page; and "Gregorio Cortez Spent Night Here En Route to Pen," *Houston Post*, January 2, 1905, pg. 5.

2   Paredes, Americo, *With A Pistol in His Hand* (Austin: University of Texas Press, 1958), pg. 97.

3   Ibid., pg. 98.

4   "Gregoria [*sic*] Cortez Given Liberty," *Houston Chronicle*, July 19, 1913, pg. 5.

5   "Restored to Sweetheart After Years in Prison," *Austin Statesman*, July 19, 1913, front page.

Chapter Twelve

"Cotton Jeans, Woolen Plaids, and Osnaburg"— The Civil War Years

"Rags were our uniform, sire! Nine out of ten of them was in rags. And it was a fighting uniform."

Valentine Bennett after the Battle of Gonzales in 1835

"Their ragged clothes make no difference. The enemy never sees the backs of my Texans."

General Robert E. Lee describing Hood's Texas Brigade thirty years later

From the preceding quotes, it is obvious that supplying military uniforms had been a chronic problem in Texas from the early years of the Republic into statehood. The sheer scale of the Civil War effort ensured that supplying the Texans enrolled in the Confederate army would be difficult if not impossible.

By 1856 the state had built a cotton and wool mill at Huntsville in order to make the penitentiary self-sustaining. The mill, which could process 500 bales of cotton and 6,000

The original facade of the Huntsville Unit featured its prominent clock tower. Today the tower is gone but the Walls Unit still features one of the old clocks in front of the building. (photo courtesy of Texas State Archives)

pounds of wool annually, did so during the Civil War to bring money into the state in an attempt to boost the failing war-time economy.

The penitentiary at Huntsville, under the control of the state government, focused on manufacturing cotton and woolen cloth and made each year over a million and a half yards of material.

The Military Board of Texas, established in 1862, was a wartime agency composed of the governor, comptroller, and treasurer with the responsibility of controlling the domestic, Confederate, and international commerce of the state.

At one point during the difficult war years, the Military Board imported forty thousand pairs of cotton and wool cards from Europe and distributed them to women throughout Texas to be used in the home manufacture of cotton and woolen cloth.

Cotton was purchased from Texas farmers and exported to Mexico with the proceeds used to buy arms, munitions, and other war supplies. The total amounts received and disbursed by this board have been estimated at two million dollars.

Although Texas was woefully short of any real established manufacturing facilities at the time of secession, the Military Board succeeded—at least marginally—in establishing several such facilities throughout the state. The most important manufacturing plant was the Texas State Penitentiary at Huntsville, which the board assigned to produce various cloth materials.

During the course of the Civil War, Texas prisoners produced considerable amounts of cotton jeans, woolen plaids, and osnaburg—a cheap but coarse, strong, unbleached cotton fabric used chiefly for sacking, footwear linings, and other heavy cloth requirements.

During the war years the penitentiary sold more than two million yards of cotton and nearly 300,000 yards of wool to both civilians and the government of the Confederate States of America. Wartime production made a profit of $800,000.[1]

In the early months of the Civil War, Texas volunteer soldiers received their initial clothing and equipment mostly from local contributions. Unit recruitment tended to be organized into community-based companies, and ladies' aid societies spun, knitted, and sewed to outfit the volunteers from their communities.

Throughout the war such household efforts were significant, and the importation of the cotton and wool cards from Europe was designed to aid in this home-based manufacturing of uniforms.

But by 1862 it was obvious the war would not end quickly, and the Confederate Quartermaster's Clothing Bureau began taking control of all clothing and equipage supply in the state.

In 1863 the Texas Legislature authorized the free distribution of cloth manufactured at the Huntsville prison to be given to families of Texas Confederate soldiers.

By January 1864 the army operated several major quartermaster depots and shops throughout Texas, but the clothing mill at the Huntsville penitentiary remained the most efficient and productive throughout the war years.

At the outbreak of the Civil War the Texas prison system was still in the developmental stage, and prison records indicate only 182 inmates in 1860. As the state implemented martial law throughout Texas, the number of criminals increased but apprehension was hampered by the lack of law enforcement officers—the majority of able-bodied men were serving in the army.

In 1864 convicts from neighboring states—Missouri, Louisiana, and Arkansas—were transferred to Huntsville to help man the textile mill.

During the war years some additional Texas criminals were processed into the prison unit at Huntsville, and some court-marshaled and convicted Confederate army prisoners were interned there. As the Confederacy began to accumulate Union prisoners, prison camps were established at various points in Texas. Most were temporary in nature—designed more as holding facilities for transfer than permanent prison camps.

Three Civil War Confederate prisons in Texas, however, were designed along more permanent lines: Camp Verde in Kerr County, Camp Ford near Tyler, and Camp Groce near Hempstead. During the course of the Red River Campaign, the facility at Camp Ford became for a period the largest prisoner-of-war camp west of the Mississippi River.

At the Huntsville state prison a number of Union prisoners began to be transferred in from the outlying prisoner-of-war facilities. Imprisonment at Huntsville was considered far preferable to internment in the military prisons such as at Camp Ford.

The first Union prisoners to be processed into Huntsville quickly found they had an unlikely friend nearby. Strolling through the front entry gates of the prison to visit them on a regular basis was no less a legendary figure than Sam Houston himself.

During these years Houston had fallen in disfavor among Texas officials and authorities and many of the citizens. When Abraham Lincoln was elected president of the United States and southern states began seceding, a movement quickly formed to withdraw Texas from the Union as well. Governor Houston, who refused to recognize the authority of the convention to take this action, refused to take an oath of allegiance to the new government, whereupon the convention removed him from office on March 16.

President Lincoln twice offered Houston the use of federal troops to keep him in office and Texas in the Union, but Houston declined and left office. While he opposed Texas withdrawing from the Union, he purchased his son a Confederate uniform when the younger Sam joined the Confederate army. The younger Houston was later wounded at the Battle of Shiloh.

In 1862 Houston moved his wife and other children to Huntsville but continued to travel around Texas. In May of that year General Paul Hebert, the Confederate military commander in the state, placed Texas under martial law. Houston, however, continued to come and go as he pleased—he was, after all, the Sword of San Jacinto, former Republic of Texas president, and former Texas governor.

One of the places he chose to visit when he felt like it was the state prison that was near his home in Huntsville. Unable to prevent him, prison and military authorities could only acquiesce, as Sam Houston would wander in through the main gate and spend hours visiting with the Union soldiers. He reportedly used his still-considerable personal influence with the authorities to procure furloughs for some of the prisoners of war so they could leave the prison and visit Huntsville.

As his health deteriorated, Houston continued to walk over to the prison and visit with the prisoners. Then on July 26, 1863, the old warrior passed away at his home in Huntsville.

In a unique wartime show of respect, Union prisoners of war being held in the Texas prison at Huntsville built a coffin scavenged from lumber found around the prison compound and, under guard, carried it up the hill to Houston's home. He was placed inside it and buried in Huntsville where his final memorial remains today.

Texas is not prominent in the maps and geography books of the Civil War. Like Arkansas and Louisiana, Texas was geographically isolated from the rest of the Confederacy by the Mississippi River even before Union forces gained control of that strategic river way. Few battles were fought on Texas soil, and the eventual Union naval blockade isolated Texas from the rest of the world.

Texas's main contributions to the Confederacy were in the forms of volunteer soldiers and war materials produced and supplied to the Southern army.

Granite monuments honoring Texas Confederates—usually constructed of pink Texas granite—can be found on virtually all of the major battlefields of the Civil War. The battlefield exploits of Texans at Vicksburg and elsewhere became almost mythical in the aftermath of the defeat of the Confederacy.

Less significant was Texas's contribution to the material needs of the Confederate war effort. For all its bravado, General Robert E. Lee's characterization of "Their ragged clothes make no difference. The enemy never sees the backs of my Texans" makes for wonderful reference and quotation but cannot disguise the fact that Texas soldiers suffered greatly due to war shortages during their campaigns.

But, for its part, the Texas prison system in Huntsville and the inmates manning the cloth mill there did more than their share to support the men at war.

1   "Prison System," *New Handbook of Texas in Six Volumes* (Austin: The Texas State Historical Association, 1996).

Chapter Thirteen

"Pardon Me, 'Ma' Did"— Miriam A. Ferguson

There was a story, unconfirmed of course, that told of Governor Miriam Amanda Ferguson visiting Rice Institute (now Rice University) in Houston and riding an elevator where one of the students accidentally stepped on her foot. Embarrassed, the student beseeched her: "Governor, I beg your pardon." Miriam Ferguson, the story goes, replied, "You will have to see my husband about that."

That tale, whether it was a story or a joke, was just one of many such references to the Fergusons' wide-open policy of pardoning convicts in the Texas prisons during her tenure as governor. Her first two-year administration in particular could be characterized as *very* lenient. At one point a convict actually escaped from a Texas prison and reported in person directly to the governor's office in Austin to request his own pardon.

Further emphasizing the "open-door" pardon policy of the Ferguson administration was the fact that her predecessor, Governor Pat Neff, had only pardoned ninety-two convicts during his entire four-year administration.

In contrast, one of Miriam Ferguson's first actions as governor was to request a list of all inmates in the state prison system who were scheduled for release in 1925 and had clear prison records. In the first seventy days of her administration, she issued 239 pardons.

Controversy was no stranger to Miriam Amanda Ferguson—referred to in the press and by Texans as "Ma" because of her first two initials. She had previously lived in the Texas governor's mansion in Austin, albeit not as the chief executive. Her husband, James Edward Ferguson, had served as Texas governor from 1915 to 1917 before being impeached by the Texas House of Representatives, convicted by the state Senate, and removed from office and declared ineligible to hold any office of trust or profit under the state.

In 1924 Miriam Ferguson ran as a candidate for governor as a proxy for her impeached husband. Apparently with her approval, James Ferguson conducted her campaign under the slogan to the voters: "Two governors for the price of one."

As she was sworn in as governor in her own right in 1925, there was little doubt that her husband—and his political skeletons—were at the power center of her administration.

James Ferguson, in his two brief years in the executive mansion, had shown an almost bizarre interest in the convicts serving time in the Texas penitentiary system. During the years of his administration, prison reform had been a hot political issue. He was convinced that the Texas prison system was corrupt, brutal, and inefficient, and as governor he had supposedly visited the Huntsville unit anonymously in civilian clothing to talk with the convicts, eat their food, and get a feel for the daily routine of Texas prisoners.

It was a fascination with prisons and prisoners that would rub off on his wife after she became governor.

Arguments and debate continue today regarding Miriam Ferguson's use of her parole powers as governor. Some within her (and Jim's) inner circle inside the governor's office felt her actions were the result of a genuine concern for the welfare of prisoners, while others within that same circle accused them both of "selling" pardons as a way of padding their incomes and accumulating considerable wealth while in office.

In 1920 the Eighteenth Amendment signaled the approval of Prohibition in Texas and the rest of the United States, and in 1925 Governor Miriam Ferguson assumed office to discover that many Texas inmates were serving two-year sentences in prison as the result of a Texas bootlegging law. While she was a strict temperance advocate, James Ferguson was far more lenient and felt that no man should be serving two years in prison for bootlegging when he could be home working and providing for his family.

Ignoring the fact that if the convict had been home working and providing for his family rather than bootlegging illegal liquor he wouldn't be in prison, the Fergusons nevertheless came to view bootleggers in prison more as victims than as criminals.

At least the supporters of Miriam Ferguson advocated this "kind-hearted" administration of justice she and James were practicing with regards to pardoning criminals from the prison system. Their critics and opponents—and there were legions of them—advocated that the administration's lenient approval of paroles was the result of financial graft. That James Ferguson had been previously impeached and convicted of charges involving graft and financial corruption only fueled the charges against "Ma and Pa" Ferguson during 1925 and 1926.

Despite wide-felt suspicions by the Texas electorate that the state prison system was in fact riddled by corruption and brutal guards and administrators, Miriam Ferguson's pardon of 239 convicted criminals in the first seventy days of her administration created a firestorm of controversy and opposition.

Almost immediately visitors waiting outside her office to see her noticed that they were vying for her time with families of prisoners and even ex-cons wanting to get their citizenship privileges restored through a pardon.

The rumors abounded—fueled in part by the whispered suspicions of state employees in and around the governor's office—that these families were "buying" pardons for their sons in the penitentiary system.

As governor, only Miriam Ferguson could sign and formalize a pardon, but much of the preparation and approvals prior to her signature were done through her husband.

One story that persisted throughout her administration told of the father of a Texas convict who was trying to approach the governor. Intervening, Jim Ferguson told the man that he and Miriam would be on the family farm that weekend and the man should visit them there and his son's future could be discussed.

The father, according to the story, arrived at the Ferguson ranch extremely distraught and anxious to negotiate his son's release from prison. To calm the man down, Jim walked him out behind the house to a fence where an old swayback horse was standing in a pen. As the two men paused at the fence, Jim Ferguson asked the man if he'd like to buy the horse for $150.

The man, already a nervous wreck, responded that he was too worried about his son to even consider buying a horse.

"That's too bad," James Ferguson reportedly told him, "because if you bought that horse, your son could ride home from Huntsville on it."[1]

No one seems to know for sure if the story's true or not—variations of it existed involving a swayback mare, a broken-down mule, and a dried-up cow—but the point of the story was always that the Fergusons, especially James, were always looking for a way to profit from selling pardons to inmates' families.

Another story tells of a prison warden calling James Ferguson and asking that a World War I veteran serving time at Huntsville be allowed a furlough to visit his sick father out of state. Even Jim Ferguson was cautious about this request: The man was a convicted murderer serving a ninety-nine-year sentence. Under those circumstances the risk was very high that the man would "rabbit"—run and never come back to Texas.

The warden, however, insisted the convict was reliable, and on that basis the furlough request was approved. After about a week the convict telephoned the governor's office and reported his father had died and another ten-day furlough would help him assist his elderly mother through the necessary funeral arrangements. Not having much choice and wanting to keep the incident out of the newspapers, James Ferguson approved the furlough extension while fearing the worst.

But as the extension neared its end, the convict appeared at the governor's office in Austin on the way back to Huntsville. The visit, he purportedly explained, was to thank Governor and Mr. Ferguson for allowing him to visit his family at such a difficult time.

This bizarre story, whether true or not, paled in comparison to another story in which a young man in his early twenties appeared with the other visitors waiting outside the governor's office one day in May of 1926.

As it was late in the afternoon, according to Miriam Ferguson's secretary Ghent Sanderford, she inquired as to the business of the remaining people waiting outside her door. Sanderford polled the visitors and reported back to James and Miriam: "office seekers, hangers on, and one escaped convict!"

The man was escorted into the governor's office and reported that he had escaped from one of the prison units the night before so he could come to Austin and ask the governor personally for a pardon.

Then, according the Sanderford, James Ferguson told the boy to report back to prison, take his punishment, and behave himself. If he fulfilled those stipulations, the governor's husband supposedly told him, a pardon would be issued the next month.

Then, if the story is true, James Ferguson took a pen and wrote a note reading: "TO ANY PEACE OFFICER IN TEXAS: The bearer of this letter is an escaped convict voluntarily returning to the penitentiary. Please do not arrest him. J.E. Ferguson." It's not known if the note was used or not, but the escapee supposedly reported back to prison, took his punishment, and received a pardon on the fourteenth of June in 1926.[2]

But Miriam Ferguson, like her husband, was not content just to sit in the executive office and process paperwork pardons for prison inmates in Texas. Like James, she wanted to meet the criminals, talk with them, eat meals with them, and truly get to know what prison life was like in Texas in the mid-1920s.

There was no way she could slip into the unit at Huntsville and meet the prisoners (as Jim claimed to have done as governor) without creating a security nightmare for prison authorities. Jim had a better idea—as later recalled by one of their two daughters.

Three miles northwest of the capitol in Austin was an old World War I military facility called Camp Mabry. At the time of Miriam Ferguson's administration, Camp Mabry consisted of nearly 400 acres and several run-down barracks and administration buildings.

James Ferguson felt this would be an ideal project in which to transfer some "honor" inmates from Huntsville to Austin in the form of a work detail to clean up Camp Mabry. It would also give the governor the opportunity to visit the inmates under controlled circumstances and get to know them.

The inmates traveled to Austin for the work detail, and Jim Ferguson went out to the camp and talked with each of them. Then, satisfied that there was no danger, he took Miriam and their two daughters out to the camp to meet the convicts. Miriam reportedly was so impressed that she ordered the governor's mansion staff to prepare food for everybody and deliver it to the camp so they could all eat supper together. That project was such a success that the governor and Jim dined each evening for a week with the prisoners.[3]

Another time, suspecting that the inmates at Camp Mabry may have been hand-picked and coached, Miriam Ferguson loaded the family into their car and drove to Huntsville. There, inside the high brick walls of the Huntsville unit, the family set up a table and chairs around a large oak tree in the prison courtyard.

Then, as a procession of inmates was brought forward one at a time, Governor Ferguson would sit and talk with each of them. "What did you do?" was always her first question. James finally asked her if it wouldn't be more diplomatic to ask them what they'd been charged with, to which Miriam answered: "If they hadn't done something, they wouldn't be here. Every one of them says he didn't do anything. If they're telling the truth, the place is full of innocent people."

It appears that the governor was able to see, where her husband couldn't, the almost universal law of convict rationale: They are innocent and shouldn't be incarcerated.

Still, she continued to sign pardons at a record pace, and if she didn't believe their stories of innocence, her critics harped, the pardons must be the result of "payoffs."

Many events—and many charges—highlighted Miriam Amanda Ferguson's two-year administration. But probably the greatest legacy of her governorship was her relationship to the prison system and the convicts inside it.

At times it appeared only those inmates with families on the outside were granted pardons, but at other times there was no rationale to her clemency. On one occasion she decided to grant pardons to seventy-five tubercular inmates, and on one Juneteenth holiday (Texas's Emancipation Day for former slaves) she granted pardons to forty-five poor, homeless black inmates.[4] Almost certainly both of these mass pardons represented inmates who could not afford "payoffs."

But sign pardons she did at a record pace. One of her final acts as governor in that term was to pardon 33 rapists, 133 murderers, 124 robbers, and 127 liquor law violators.[5] The fact that violent offenders made up two-thirds of those pardons cast suspicion on the theory that her clemency was in reaction to what she saw as "an unfairly administered bootlegging law."

Miriam Ferguson lost her bid for re-election after that term but later ran again on several occasions and, in 1933, was successful in achieving a second term as Texas governor. That term, from 1933 to 1935, did not see the earlier emphasis on pardoning Texas prison inmates. That second term did, however, have a resounding impact on the Texas prison system in another fashion.

In protest to her re-election and the charges of graft and corruption during her first administration, many law officers in Texas resigned in protest. One of those turning in his badge was the highly regarded Texas Ranger named Frank Hamer.

In January of 1934 Clyde Barrow and Bonnie Parker led a bloody assault on a prison work force at the Eastham Unit that resulted in the escape of four convicts and the murder of two prison guards including a field major. The director of the Texas prison system, Lee Simmons, swore vengeance and hand-picked the man he wanted to track down and capture Bonnie and Clyde: dead or alive.

But first Simmons had to convince the governor's office to create and legalize a new state government position—that of Special Investigator for the Texas Prison System. And the man he chose to fill the position was the former ranger who had resigned in protest of the Ferguson's re-election to the office of governor: Frank Hamer.

Miriam Ferguson, however, was also horrified at the bloody Eastham raid and approved the position—and Hamer —and signed the executive order into law.

Hamer proved to be the right man for the job. Only 102 days after he was assigned the position, both Clyde Barrow and Bonnie Parker lay dead on a backwoods Louisiana road. So, in a sense, Miriam Ferguson gave back to the Texas prison system as well as she took from it.

She did not seek re-election after that second term but did run unsuccessfully one last time in 1940. The rumors of great wealth amassed due to the selling of pardons and her husband's involvement in Texas politics during her first administration apparently were vastly overstated. After her second term the Fergusons lost their ranch to bankruptcy and were hounded by IRS agents trying to collect back taxes.

But she will always be best remembered for her first administration and her lenient pardon policy. By the end of that term, in 1927, she had signed 3,595 acts of executive clemency including 1,318 full pardons and 829 conditional pardons—statistics unlikely to ever be matched again by the Texas governor's office.

It remains today her legacy with the Texas prison system.

And, unlike the unfortunate student at Rice Institute, begging her pardon in the 1920s could be very profitable. Just for whom and to what extent remains a matter of conjecture.

1   Paulissen, May Nelson and Carl McQueary, *Miriam: The Southern Belle Who Became the First Woman Governor of Texas* (Austin: Eakin Press, 1995), pg. 159.
2   Ibid., pp. 158-159.
3   Ibid., pg. 152.
4   Ibid., pg. 163.
5   Abernethy, Francis Edward, ed., *Legendary Ladies of Texas* (Dallas: E-Heart Press, 1981), pg. 156.

Governor Miriam A. Ferguson is today honored and buried in the Texas State Cemetery, but her lenient pardon and parole policies led to charges of corruption and graft. She presided over Texas during a period of extreme turmoil in the state prison system during the 1930s. (photo by Gary Brown)

As this plaque in Austin attests, Governor Miriam Ferguson was attacked for her liberal pardoning policy. She is buried today with her husband in the Texas State Cemetery and remains a controversial figure. (photo by Gary Brown)

Chapter Fourteen

"Singing a Lonesome Song"—The Texas State Railroad

Well, if they freed me from this prison, if that railroad train
was mine, I bet I'd move on over a little farther down the line.

Folsom Prison Blues John R. Cash; © 1956 Hi Lo Music

Prison lore, railroads, and convict dreams have always seemed to be intertwined. Perhaps it is the train's sorrowful whistle and distant inaccessibility that has made it so prominent in inmate stories and music.

Huddie Ledbetter, or Leadbelly, made "Midnight Special" a blues standard, in part from his experiences at the Sugarland Unit. Johnny Cash tried to sing from an inmate's point of view in "Folsom Prison Blues."

Both songs emphasize the vision of the train as an avenue of escape from daily prison life. Referring to distant trains, Leadbelly sang "You know, if I ever get to jumpin' Oh Lord, I'll up and jump away" while Cash sang "I bet I'd move on over a little farther down the line."

Likewise, Cash recorded "When I hear that whistle blowin' I hang my head and cry," and Huddie Ledbetter sang "I heard that special, Singing a lonesome song."

Trains and inmate prisoners in Texas share far more than music lore, however. From the time of Reconstruction until the early twentieth century, the Texas prison system was heavily involved in the development of railroads. Almost every major railroad system that laid track in Texas after the Civil War found a readily available source of cheap labor by leasing convicts from the state prison system.

Convict labor provided the cutting and hewing of early railway ties, bridge materials, and construction of water towers. Land, often in the worst of conditions, was cleared, track laid, and railheads built—in large part by inmate labor for which the wealthy railroads usually paid Texas only pennies per day per convict.

While convict leasing extended to nearly all major industries in post-war Texas, the very first leases came about in 1867, when two railroad companies headquartered in the state hired prison inmates to help construct their roadbeds. Soon nearly every railroad in the state had followed suit.

Because railroads spurred the development of communities along the main lines, the use of inmate labor often brought the prisoners within close proximity of the townspeople, who often resented and feared the presence of convicted criminals. And, too, reports kept surfacing of gross abuse of the inmates by the prison guards and railroad administrators who were responsible for feeding and boarding them.

In 1879 the *Wood County Flag* reported that a nearby prison camp responsible for cutting cross ties consisted of inmates who were completely at the mercy of guards who were "heartless brutes in the shape of men" and guilty of "unnecessary cruelty, brutish treatment, and outrageous conduct toward the convicts."[1] Of course part of the *Flag*'s indignation may have been the result of opposition by the local men at having paying jobs denied them by inmates.

But nowhere in Texas were prison inmates more connected in railroad development than in East Texas with the Rusk Penitentiary and the Texas State Railroad. The Texas State Railroad, in fact, was initially operated by the Texas Prison Commission. Mostly built by inmate labor, the railroad has changed hands, ceased operation, reopened several times, faltered many times, but is today still operated as the Texas State Railroad State Historical Park. Inmate involvement in its development extended into the 1970s.

Ironically, the Texas State Railroad was the indirect result of overcrowding at the Huntsville Penitentiary. To remedy the shortage of secure, walled prison housing, the Rusk Penitentiary was built between 1877 and 1883. When completed, the state's second walled prison for convicted felons quickly overshadowed the established headquarters at Huntsville.

The Rusk Penitentiary consisted of a three-story administration building and a two-story cellblock larger than the one at Huntsville. It also hosted a chapel, hospital, and library—considered "progressive" for the 1880s. By 1888 Rusk had been equipped with a 300-kilowatt power plant—some two years before electricity was introduced at Huntsville.

But the choice of Rusk—located in the East Texas piney woods—was largely based upon the speculation that convict labor could be used to develop the newly discovered iron-ore resources in that area. To that end, iron foundries and a blast furnace were installed.

When the prison was initially opened in 1883 it was leased to a private organization, but the penitentiary-lease program was ended that same year. In 1884 Texas leased the prison's iron industry to the Comer and Faris Company with the agreement that one thousand inmates would be made available and the state would be reimbursed for their labor based upon their skill levels.

A twenty-five-ton blast furnace—fueled by charcoal—was installed and named the "Old Alcalde." It never performed up to expectations, and a shutdown was ordered after only two months. Modifications were made and the furnace re-fired, but it too failed to produce as hoped, and a second shutdown was ordered in September whereupon Comer and Faris canceled their contract with the state. A larger fifty-ton coke-burning furnace would later be installed.

At this point the Texas State Railroad might never have developed. But Texas prison officials were determined to make the iron industry into a profitable venture by providing iron products throughout Texas, its neighboring states, and south into Mexico. And such plans would include transportation requirements.

To salvage the industry at Rusk, the Texas Nineteenth Legislature appropriated $50,000 to establish the iron industry on state account. Outside consultants were brought in, and by November 1886 the blast furnace was producing full time and beginning to show a profit.

The state made a contract with itself for the Rusk Penitentiary to provide the cast-iron work for the new capitol building being constructed in Austin. Inmates would be producing an estimated two million pounds of iron structural works, including the dome structure and ornamentation for the new building.

Texas prison inmates at the Rusk Penitentiary manufactured this detailed ornamental work for the state capitol building. (photo by Gary Brown)

Inmates at the Rusk Penitentiary manufactured this ornamental ironwork for the Texas State Capitol during the 1880s. (photo by Gary Brown)

The stone contracts for the capitol had required inmate labor to construct narrow-gauge railroads to transport the granite—one from the Oatmanville quarry to Austin and one from Granite Mountain to Marble Falls. Both rail projects proved to be successful, and when the Rusk iron industry needed a railway, convicts were again chosen as a cheap, readily available source of labor.

The Texas prison system began construction of the Texas State Railroad in 1896. That year the first five miles of track was cleared and built from North Rusk

Inmates produced the finely detailed cast-iron supports found throughout the Texas State Capitol in the Texas prison system. (photo by Gary Brown)

and extended west to the penitentiary compound specifically to haul iron ore to the prison blast furnace. The prison system could now ship finished cast-iron products from the unit to the commercial railheads located at Rusk.

When the fifty-ton, coke-burning second blast furnace became operational in 1903, it was decided to use inmates to extend the railroad tracks another five miles to the community of Maydelle. As this construction was going on, the legislature decided to make the Texas State Railroad a common carrier and extend the rail line all the way to Palestine where it could make connections with the numerous national railroad companies operating from and through that city.

Reports similar to those of the 1879 *Wood County Flag* extra edition began to surface regarding the working conditions of the convicts being used on the Maydelle line. Reformers complained about the mortality rates and working conditions that accompanied the construction of the road, describing it as "stained with the blood of some helpless convict man or boy lashed cruelly by a savage prison guard or sergeant."[2]

Nevertheless, convict labor continued to extend the tracks, and the Maydelle railhead was completed in 1906. By 1909 the tracks reached Palestine, and the Texas prison system had succeeded in its plan of connecting the Rusk Penitentiary with the industrial railheads some thirty-two miles away.

The prisoners who built those thirty-two miles of tracks through often hostile land had done so at a cost to Texas of just over $500,000.

Complaints by prison reform advocates were usually well founded. The inmates worked brutal schedules—usually sunrise to dusk—year round. Room and board was subsistence in most cases, and injuries and mutilations were commonplace. Reports persisted of unmarked inmate graves lining the tracks through the woods.

The economic depression of 1907 dramatically reduced the sale of iron products, and the prison closed the foundry in 1913. Although the concept of using the railroad to ship prison foundry products at a profit never really materialized, the Texas State Railroad did manage to operate marginally in the black because of passenger service and the availability of connecting railroads at Palestine.

Prisoners made up the train crew, except for the engineer. When a passenger service was extended to Palestine, a full-time staff of nine was employed.

After the closing of the foundry in 1913, Rusk Penitentiary attempted to manufacture other products such as bricks, wagons, brooms, and mattresses, but those enterprises also failed and the prison was closed in 1917. In 1918 it was reopened as an insane asylum named the Rusk State Hospital.

One final attempt to make a go of the iron works occurred when a Beaumont company purchased the foundry in 1919, but when that business also failed, the plant reverted back to Texas in 1929 and was dismantled in 1931.

By 1921 the Texas State Railroad was also failing financially, and the legislature appropriated $150,000 to upgrade the tracks and equipment and lease the facilities to the Texas and New Orleans Railroad, which operated a Pullman service but primarily used the tracks to ship lumber products.

In 1962 the Texas and New Orleans was incorporated into the Southern Pacific Railroad Company and leased to the Texas Southeastern Railroad Company until 1969. At that time the Missouri Pacific leased a few miles of the track, and in 1970 an unsuccessful attempt was made by the Cherokee and Southwestern Tourist Railroad Corporation to resume passenger service. The Texas State Railroad had died.

The Sixty-first Texas Legislature assigned the land to the Texas Parks and Wildlife Department in 1972 for development as a hiking and bike trail. Private groups and government officials, however, urged the development of one last effort to save the old rail line, and the Texas State Railroad State Historical Park was created.

Steam locomotives and other turn-of-the-century rail equipment were located throughout the United States, and once again Texas convicts were utilized to upgrade the tracks, bridges, and other facilities.

There is an irony in the fact that, nearly one hundred years after Texas prison inmates began laying track for the Rusk Penitentiary, convicted felons from the penitentiaries would once again be used to rebuild the original lines.

This time there was no convict lease system. Work conditions, safety precautions, and food were far better in the 1970s.

And while convicts had succeeded in building the railroad in the late 1800s, Texas inmates also succeeded in refurbishing it in the late 1900s. They rebuilt the line, cleared brush, shored up bridges, and replaced rails and ties.

On the nation's Bicentennial observance on July 4, 1976, the park was opened to the public and today offers passenger service on restored steam locomotives operating out of train stations in both Palestine and Rusk.

In the 1920s Leadbelly may well have rested in his cell at night and listened to the "lonesome song" of the Midnight Special whistling as it passed through Sugarland out of Houston. The thought creates a somber and sorrowful image at the impossible longing of an inmate to escape the hell of his confinement.

As Johnny Cash wrote and sang, "I bet there's rich folk eatin' in a fancy dining car. They're prob'ly drinkin' coffee and smokin' big cigars."

Yes, the disappearing passenger trains with their sleeping compartments and dining cars also conjure up images of relative ease and luxury on the railroad tracks.

But you can also imagine how that relative ease and luxury came at a tremendous cost to those Texas convicts in post-Civil War Texas who struggled sunup to sundown to lay those railroad tracks through Texas heat, humidity, mosquitoes, and even "blue northers."

In a sense, the Texas State Railroad State Historical Park is their memorial today.

1   *Wood County Flag*, Extra, June 28, 1879, p. 1 quoted in Walker, Donald R., *Penology for Profit: A History of the Texas Prison System 1867-1912* (College Station: Texas A&M University Press, 1988), pg. 58.

2   "Texas State Railroad," *New Handbook of Texas in Six Volumes* (Austin: The Texas State Historical Association, 1996).

Chapter Fifteen

"The Texas Prison Houdini"– Charles Frazier

In 1906 the custodian of the United States Jail in Washington, D.C., Warden James H. Harris, wrote a letter certifying that Harry Houdini had been stripped of all clothing, searched, and locked in a secure cell of the national jail. Within two minutes Houdini escaped his cell, broke into another cell where his clothing was kept, and opened the rest of the cell doors on the South Wing within twenty-one minutes.

That probably remains some kind of record in some book somewhere, and Houdini is still today considered one of the best, if not the greatest, escape artist in history.

But before Harry Houdini's death in New York City in 1926, another escape artist had begun developing prison cell escape skills in Texas prisons. Before he was finished, this Texas convict would set all kinds of records for escapes. But this trickster didn't rely upon skill, endurance, or illusions.

Charlie Frazier, Inmate #54953, took a more simple approach to breaking out of prison cells: He usually shot his way out, and if people got killed—whether it be guards or other inmates—so be it. And before his career ended, a considerable body count could be attributed to him.

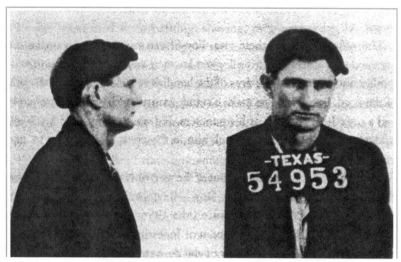

Charlie Frazier, 1934. Frazier was mastermind of the escape from the death house. (photo courtesy of the Texas Prison Archives, Criminal Justice, Institutional Division [TDCJ-ID])

Charlie Frazier successfully escaped from prisons in Texas, Arkansas, and Louisiana on at least a dozen occasions. His exploits included the successful and bloody mass escape from Angola Prison in Louisiana and the only successful escape from the Texas Death House. That incident resulted in the escape of Joe Palmer, Raymond Hamilton, and Blackie Thompson from death cells, but Frazier himself was seriously wounded inside the prison.

Frazier was born in 1897 and first arrived at Huntsville on January 13, 1917, when he was just barely twenty years old. He was processed in that day after his conviction in Red River County for a criminal habit that would plague him all of his adult life: burglary.

Within seven months he would make his first successful escape only to be captured two days later. The following year, 1918, he escaped in January and remained free for nearly eight months until he was arrested in Hugo, Oklahoma. When Oklahoma authorities returned him to Huntsville, he escaped the day he arrived only to be immediately recaptured.

From October of 1918 until February 23, 1920, he remained in custody in Texas prisons due, possibly, to the fact his sentence was up on that date. Texas obviously at that time did not consider prison escape a felony offense punishable by additional time as it does today.

This young criminal had in the first eighteen months of his three-year sentence managed to escape three times. While it didn't get him additional time, it did deny him any chance at early parole, and he served his complete three-year sentence before discharging.

He had only been a free man a few months when he was arrested in Arcadia, Louisiana, and convicted of robbery and burglary. This time he received a sentence of eight to ten years in the Louisiana State Penitentiary.

Louisiana seems to have had better luck keeping him behind cell bars than Texas—at least initially. Frazier paroled out on July 1, 1922, after serving only twenty-five months on an eight-to-ten-year sentence.

In less than four months he was arrested again for burglary—this time in Oberlin, Louisiana—and quickly returned to the Louisiana State Penitentiary with a new four-year sentence. Although just twenty-five years old, he had already earned three separate prison sentences in Texas and Louisiana. The pattern for the remainder of his adult life had been established, and he would never really be a free man again until his death in 1959. Well, not really free except for his many brief periods of freedom after escapes.

Again, it would appear that Louisiana had figured out how to keep this convict safely behind bars as he served his time without incident through three years. Then on December 4, 1925, he escaped from the Louisiana prison system.

Until this time Charlie Frazier had been a petty criminal catching relatively short terms for robbery and burglary crimes that had not resulted in death or injury to others. All that changed in 1926.

While Louisiana authorities were searching for him, Frazier was arrested in Marion County, Texas, and charged with robbery with firearms, burglary, and theft over $50. This crime had involved weapons, and this Texas jury wasn't in the mood for leniency: Frazier headed back to Huntsville with a twenty-five-year sentence.

His prison records from that return indicate he was five foot ten and weighed 153 pounds, which would have made him an average sized inmate—indicating his meanness and toughness came from his demeanor rather than any intimidating physical presence.

Unusual for convicts of his background was the fact he had no tattoos recorded upon entering Huntsville. Small brown moles were noted on his upper right arm, lower right leg, and right hip. Ironically, he listed his occupation as "farmer"— something that probably got him assigned directly to field-work in prison. At his time of processing he claimed seven years of school and the ability to read and write.

One possible explanation for his claiming to be a farm worker is the fact that he didn't intend to do *any* kind of work for the Texas prison system. Within a month he had escaped again.

A week after his successful escape he returned to the same prison in the middle of the night and killed a guard while releasing six other inmates. In November of that year he was arrested in Columbia, Tennessee, and extradited to Texas. He was never charged in the murder of the Texas guard or for facilitating the escape since the only non-inmate witness was dead.

He had been back at Huntsville less than a year when, on October 13, 1927, he escaped again only to be recaptured the same day. Ten weeks later, on Christmas Day, he escaped and left the state.

While he was quickly gaining legendary status as a prison escape artist, Charlie Frazier was unable to capitalize on his skills and invariably found himself back in a prison cell somewhere. This time it was in Arkansas on July 27, 1928.

If his petty burglaries had become more violent in nature, his killing of the Texas prison guard had also spawned a newer, more aggressive side of Charlie Frazier. This time he was assessed a life sentence for murder of a police officer in Little River, Arkansas, and it was that state's turn to try to keep him confined.

He must have been a model prisoner initially in Arkansas, for after two and a half years Governor Hanley Parnell commuted his life sentence to twenty-one years. Exactly why Governor Parnell decided on leniency toward Charlie Frazier is unknown, but the act was signed during the Christmas season on December 23, 1931.

Exactly one year to the day later, on December 23, 1932, Governor Parnell in an incredibly risky move approved and signed a fifteen-day Christmas furlough for Frazier.

Charlie never returned.

But again, it was less than four months before he was arrested again—this time back in Louisiana—and sent to the maximum security Louisiana prison at Angola. It appeared that correctional authorities were finally learning that Charlie Frazier had become an incorrigible and violent criminal.

This time Frazier had been arrested in Benton, Louisiana, and convicted of robbery and shooting with intent to murder. Like the Texas jury previously in Marion County, this panel of Louisiana jurors let it be known they were tired of dealing with Charlie Frazier: He was sentenced to life in prison plus eighteen to twenty years and the remainder of his sentence from which he'd escaped in 1925.

Now Charlie Frazier, who had already established himself as an escape artist, found himself faced with the rest of his life behind prison bars and nothing to lose by continuing his escape attempts. His escape history, however, assured he would be kept in maximum security, and therefore any future escapes would by necessity be violent attempts. The year 1933 would mark the transition of Charlie Frazier into one of the most violent and unmanageable prisoners in the American South, if not the entire nation.

Angola, with its horrendous reputation, would seem to have been a secure assignment for Charlie Frazier.

But Charlie Frazier had also developed a horrendous reputation by this time. In sixteen years, since his first incarceration in Texas, he had been convicted of more than a dozen crimes—many violent—and had escaped at least nine times from state prisons in Texas, Louisiana, and Arkansas.

It would take him less than five months to make his first move.

The Mississippi River surrounds Angola Prison on three sides. Guards would often drag a captured alligator into the prison compound and kill it and let it rot near the inmate quarters as a reminder of what was beyond the prison perimeter should any of them try to escape. More often than not, however, it was simply the rapid, swirling waters of the river that either drowned escapees or else dumped them on the opposite bank half-dead where authorities could pick them up and return them to the prison.

The summer of 1933 had been a hot, dry season, and that September the waters were flowing lower than usual. On the second weekend of September, Saturday visitation had taken place as scheduled and a baseball game was scheduled inside Angola Prison on Sunday.

An inmate had his girlfriend smuggle in a small-caliber weapon, or weapons, during the Saturday visitation. Then, during the Sunday baseball game when the entire prison compound was distracted, the convict pulled the gun on the captain of the guard and ordered him to open the front gate of the prison. Some reports claim that only one inmate had a gun; others claim that Frazier was also armed. Perhaps there was only one gun and the inmate had given it to Frazier for the escape attempt.

The captain of the guard refused to open the gate and was killed. In the ensuing gun battle between inmates and guards, several inmates were shot and one killed. But Frazier and ten other convicts managed to escape Angola Prison in the bloodiest incident in that prison's bloody history.

The escapees got to the Mississippi River at a time when the water was low, found a log and floated down the river to a sandbar, and made it safely to the other side.

Because eleven escaped convicts would be easy to spot by trackers, they agreed to divide up. In an act that was typical of the callous, vicious convict Charles Frazier had become, he intentionally directed some of his fellow inmates to a point where he knew they'd be caught, making it possible for him to escape while they were being apprehended. Of the original eleven escapees, seven were eventually killed by authorities—many of them "resisting arrest."

Frazier and the other three headed toward northern Louisiana and embarked on a crime spree, robbing banks in Louisiana, Arkansas, and Texas. The violent mass escape at Angola remains today the worst such incident in Louisiana prison history.

But again, Charlie Frazier would not go into seclusion or hiding to let the heat fade. Within two months of the Angola prison break, on November 8, 1933, he arrived at the gates of the Texas prison in Huntsville again.

Without question, he would have faced the electric chair had he been returned to Louisiana after the Angola shootout and killing of the captain of the guard.

He managed to avoid extradition to Louisiana by negotiating a plea that guaranteed he would be sentenced to a Texas, not Louisiana, prison for the rest of his life. Actually that sentence was a multiple commitment: a two-to-ten-year sentence, a five-to-ten-year sentence, a five-to-twenty-five-year sentence, and a life sentence. Charlie Frazier was scheduled to remain inside the Texas prison system for the remainder of his natural life.

The plea bargain that kept him from returning to Louisiana would come back to haunt Texas prison officials.

Lee Simmons, director of the Texas prisons at the time, later wrote that he "had ventured a talk with Frazier" and that the man held responsible for the recent bloody Angola escape had assured him "they would have no trouble with him."[1]

In a move that rivals Arkansas Governor Parnell's granting of Frazier a Christmas furlough for stupidity, Simmons released Charlie Frazier into the general inmate population at Huntsville. Despite the fact Frazier had previously escaped from Huntsville several times in addition to escapes from Arkansas and Louisiana and the shootout at Angola, Simmons chose to allow Frazier free access to the entire inside perimeter of the Huntsville unit.

It took him two months to make his first escape attempt.

Using a homemade key, he jimmied the lock on his cell, removed bars from a cellblock window, and had crossed the prison yard headed for one of the massive brick prison walls before he was discovered.

Still, Simmons made no move to place Frazier under the special security measures his escape history would have dictated. Two days later, on January 16, 1934, Clyde Barrow and Bonnie Parker participated in a raid on the Eastham Camp

One farm unit that had resulted in the death of two guards and escape of four inmates.

The Angola mass escape had thrust the Louisiana prison system into the national headlines in 1933; the Eastham mass escape thrust the Texas prison system into the national headlines in 1934. Despite the fact the Louisiana escape had freed far more inmates, the Texas raid was particularly infamous because the notorious Bonnie and Clyde had been responsible.

Simmons swore personal vengeance in responding to the Eastham raid, and perhaps because of that he was preoccupied with it during this period. But back in Huntsville, Charlie Frazier continued to mix and mingle freely with the general inmate population.

On March 9, less than two months after his first attempt, he again escaped the cellblock, unchained a ladder, and had placed it against the wall when a guard detected him and shot him. The wound was serious but not life-threatening.

On May 23 Texas Prison Special Investigator Frank Hamer led a group of lawmen in a successful ambush of Clyde Barrow and Bonnie Parker in Louisiana, and as the summer of 1934 arrived it appeared the crises involving prisons in Texas and Louisiana had been diffused. Charlie Frazier was locked up in Texas, and Bonnie and Clyde were dead in Louisiana.

Lee Simmons had been rocked by the bad publicity of the Eastham raid under his prison administration, and that summer he took a number of steps to restore the public's faith in the state prison system. One public relations tactic was to field a prison baseball team and invite outside semi-pro teams into the prison compound at Huntsville to play before the inmates and selected sports writers around the state.

It was during just such a game between the Sun Oilers of Brenham and the Prison Tigers that Charlie Frazier made his next move.

In a scenario that eerily resembles the Angola escape attempt, the entire Huntsville prison unit was preoccupied with the ballgame being played that day.

The day before the game, July 21, Simmons claimed that an inmate tipped him off about a tunnel being dug beneath the prison print shop on Sundays when the prison industries were closed down.

Since the baseball game was being played on Sunday, Simmons and another officer waited until the game had started then raided the print shop and found that in fact a tunnel was being dug underground. On the way to the print shop, Simmons later recalled, he saw Charlie Frazier sitting by himself in the chapel.

Just why Lee Simmons would allow the most notorious escape artist in the nation to move through the Huntsville general inmate population virtually unsupervised defies explanation. Less than two months earlier Frazier had made his second attempt to scale the walls in as many months, and yet in July he was wandering around the nearly vacated prison compound unguarded during the ballgame.

As he was removing the tunneling inmates to solitary confinement, Simmons came across Charlie Frazier walking alone in the yard. Later he suspected that Frazier had been armed during that brief encounter.

Simmons was at first surprised at the fact Frazier had not been involved in the underground tunneling attempt; then he recognized that the discovery had provided a perfect diversion for Charlie Frazier that afternoon. In fact, given his use of fellow escapees after the Angola escape to divert attention away from him, it is easy to wonder if he was responsible for Simmons being given the tip of the escape in progress at the print shop.

But immediately after Simmons returned to the baseball game, shots rang out and it was discovered that Charlie

Frazier had arranged to have a .45-caliber pistol smuggled into the prison. Using it to commandeer a guard with death row cell keys, Frazier freed two death row convicts—Joe Palmer and Blackie Thompson—and offered to release anybody else on death row who wanted out. Raymond Hamilton and two other prisoners did so.

In a furious firefight with guards, the six convicts made their way into the prison yard and, with a tall ladder stolen from the paint shop, began to scale the wall near a guard tower.

Guards again opened fire. Hamilton, Palmer, and Thompson made it over the wall and escaped. One of the other inmates was killed, and Frazier and another inmate were wounded and captured. It remains the only *successful* death row escape in Texas history, and again, it was Charlie Frazier who had initiated and executed the escape with his smuggled pistol.

Like Angola the year before, Huntsville now was in the national headlines for a Charlie Frazier-led mass escape from a maximum security prison—death row, no less. The fact that two of the escapees—Hamilton and Palmer—were former Barrow gang members who had escaped during the Eastham raid by Bonnie and Clyde seven months earlier made the furor even greater.

But unlike Angola, Charlie Frazier did not make it over the wall this time. And once again he was wounded—this time there was serious doubt he would survive.

But he did, and after his release from the prison hospital, he was assigned to 7 Level maximum security. Despite the fact he had not been sentenced to death row, Simmons finally placed him in just such a cell. It appears Lee Simmons finally, after two successful high-profile raids on his prison units, began to take security seriously.

Simmons had powerful enemies and critics of the prison system in high political circles and among some press reporters. Rumors circulated throughout Texas that fall concerning the treatment Frazier was receiving in solitary on death row. Some inmates claimed he was being fed only bread and water and denied bathing, haircut, and shaving privileges.

Simmons denied all charges except the loss of shaving privileges, using the rationale that a bearded Frazier would stand out in a crowd on the outside if he escaped again. But the rumors continued to circulate, fed in part by *Houston Press* reports. Later inmates Ralph Fults and Clyde Thompson would both claim that Simmons' incarceration of Frazier during that period bordered on sadistic. Thompson claimed that Frazier was welded into his cell on death row during that period and not even allowed to bathe for nearly sixteen months.[2]

That fall Simmons would resign as prison director. Simmons' successor, Dave Nelson, had Frazier removed from the death cells and transferred to a new work camp established on the Eastham farm and began negotiating with Louisiana, which wanted to extradite Frazier. In Louisiana, Frazier knew he would be tried for murder of the guard killed during the Angola escape and the prosecutor there would seek the death penalty.

At Eastham he had nothing to lose with Louisiana extradition—and a possible death penalty—ahead of him. According to Clyde Thompson, who was assigned to the same work crew as Frazier, the escape artist on two occasions had guns brought into the Eastham farm only to be thwarted at the last moment before he could spring his escape. In one, a mounted "high rider" found the weapons before the inmates did, and in the other the convict who picked up the hidden guns to carry them to Frazier instead took off on his own and was killed.[3]

On October 6, 1936, Frazier was extradited to Louisiana.

But Charlie Frazier was still not finished as an escape artist. Even before his trial began, he made another escape attempt. Lee Simmons' autobiography includes one final escape attempt, reported in an Associated Press clipping:

Charlie Frazier Still A Problem

Baton Rouge, La., Oct. 18 [1936] (AP)—With six new bullet holes in him and a leaden slug in one lung, Charlie Frazier, famed Texas desperado, will remain a "major problem" to the penitentiary officials at Angola, Warden D. D. Bazer said yesterday.

Frazier, who was shot in an attempted prison break last Friday, was sitting up this morning and will be out of the penitentiary hospital in a week or ten days, the warden said. Bazer said Frazier, who led a prison break in Angola in 1933, in which three persons were killed, is unchanged by his experience.

"I believe he'll make another attempt the first chance he gets," the warden declared.

Bazer said the one-time leader of Angola's "Red Hat" Gang was shot six times, instead of three, as first reported, suffering wounds in the back, in the chest near the heart, three in the abdomen and one in the hip.

Four of his wounds were received at close range when he tried to snatch the pistol of a guard riding with him in a truck, the warden said.

The outlaw, serving a life sentence for shooting with intent to murder, plus an additional 18-to-28 year term for burglary, has figured in prison escapes in both Texas and Arkansas.[4]

The Associated Press reported that "four of his wounds were received at close range when he tried to snatch the pistol of a guard." But Clyde Thompson later reported that the inmate grapevine (which has historically been terribly unreliable) claimed Frazier was the target of an assassination attempt by Louisiana prison guards in revenge for the murder of one of their own at Angola.

At any rate, after he healed from his gunshot wounds that time, he was in fact tried for the murder of the guard during the Angola escape. He somehow managed a hung jury and avoided the death penalty but received life in prison once more.

This time Louisiana officials made no attempts to cover up the fact that the doors to his cell were welded shut and remained so for eight years. If the commode inside had plumbing problems, parts were handed through the bars and Frazier made the repairs himself. Food was passed to him daily and water was ladled into a bucket he kept inside his cell.

Finally, with steel brackets welded across the lock of his cell, prison authorities had found a way to thwart the "Texas Prison Houdini." He never made another escape attempt. In all, he served twelve years in solitary confinement.

Then, with his health failing, an elderly Charlie Frazier found himself facing death in the only home he'd ever really known as an adult—prison. Bitterness and vindictiveness set in.

A group of Gideons visited solitary confinement cells at Angola around 1956, and as they approached Frazier, he sat on his bunk and screamed insults and obscenities at them. By this time the welded braces on his door had been cut open, and one of the Gideons went inside to talk with him.

Frazier ordered the man out of his cell but accepted the free Bible being offered. Within days he had experienced a religious conversion, and like John Wesley Hardin in the Texas prison system many years earlier, Frazier eventually became the superintendent of the Sunday school classes at Angola.

His health continued to worsen, and he was diagnosed with cancer. In his final days he was transferred to a New Orleans hospital, and prison officials, having been burned too many times by Charlie Frazier, ordered him handcuffed and shackled to his bed despite the fact he was in the terminal stages of his illness.

The Gideon who had given him the Bible learned of his situation and intervened with the Louisiana governor and attorney general and obtained permission to remove the cuffs and shackles.

When Charlie Frazier died in 1959, he left his few earthly belongings to the Gideon who had befriended him.

Charlie Frazier was a violent man who killed without conscience and made no attempts during his adult life to rehabilitate himself. Much of his life was spent in prisons outside of Texas, but the fact remains that probably no inmate in America had escaped, attempted escapes, and been shot during escapes more times than had the "Texas Houdini"—Charlie Frazier.

1   Simmons, *Assignment Huntsville*, pg. 150.
2   Umphrey, *The Meanest Man in Texas*, pg. 170.
3   Ibid., pp. 172-176.
4   Simmons, pp. 170-171.

Chapter Sixteen

"Black Bottom" and "Eighth of January"— Music to Die For

"Idle hands are the devil's tools" is an old axiom prison wardens and administrators have sworn by since the first prisoners were incarcerated at Huntsville.

Historically, work has been the institutional answer: Work the convicts all day until they're too tired at night to do anything but sleep. In the earliest days of Texas prison administration, before electricity, few recreational outlets were available for inmates other than donated reading material—usually religious tracts and complimentary Bibles.

By 1922, however, commercial radio broadcasting began in Texas, and in the earliest days before federal regulation of the airwaves, twenty-five commercial stations were in operation in the state. Among them were WBAP, Fort Worth; KGNC, Amarillo; WFAA, Dallas; WOAI, San Antonio; KFJZ, Fort Worth; KILE, Galveston; and WACO, Waco.

Radio Station WBAP in Fort Worth, in particular, made the most profound change in Texas prison inmate recreational off-hours relaxation. In many ways WBAP has historically been the flagship radio station in Texas—establishing a format for country music variety show broadcasting that was later adopted by Nashville's "Grand Ole Opry."

199

In 1932 the "Grand Ole Opry" broadcasts played a role in a bizarre game of "musical chairs" in the Texas Death House involving the electric chair Old Sparky.

But in the earliest days of radio broadcasting in Texas, almost immediately inmate-rigged antennas were pointed so as to pick up WBAP broadcasting, and prison officials used access to radio programming as a reward tool for good behavior on the cellblocks and tanks.

By 1938 radio broadcasting was in the "Golden Age of Radio" and well established throughout Texas. That year WBAP began broadcasting a weekly program called "Thirty Minutes Behind the Walls" that featured an all-prisoner cast and ran for several years.

The "Thirty Minutes Behind the Walls" program had two purposes: entertain and inform inmates in the Texas prisons and serve as a public relations instrument to develop a more favorable image of the Texas prison system with the public listeners around the state.

The "Thirty Minutes Behind the Walls" programming was an offshoot of the image-improving designs of prison director Lee Simmons in the early 1930s when he initiated the Texas Prison Rodeo and prison vs. semi-pro baseball games.

Keeping inmates informed of prison events actually started before "Thirty Minutes Behind the Walls" programming. During the famous 1935 double header between the Huntsville Prison Tigers and Brenham Sun Oilers at Houston's Buff Stadium, a special line was established so a prison officer could relay inning-by-inning results back to inmates assembled at the Huntsville Unit.

It wasn't exactly sports-radio broadcasting, but it was probably the first live "feed" directed at an inmate audience in Texas. The 1938 "Thirty Minutes Behind the Walls" programming, however, was conducted by inmates and directed at both "free-world" and inmate radio listening audiences.

The Golden Age of Radio was, after all, characterized by duos of wacky characters doing routines to entertain kids and adults gathered around those large, bulky old-time tube radios of the 1930s. It was a period of Abbott and Costello, Amos and Andy, Lum and Abner, and Fathead and Soupbone.

Yes, Fathead and Soupbone. By 1939 the Texas Prison Rodeo had become a statewide tourist event, and one of the most popular routines during the halftime entertainment was a duo of rodeo clowns named Charlie Jones and Louie Nettles. In rodeo clown costumes, they performed a routine they dubbed "Fathead and Soupbone."

In 1939, the year after "Thirty Minutes Behind the Walls" had begun broadcasting through WBAP, the public began writing the prison officials in Huntsville, requesting that Fathead and Soupbone do their routines during the thirty-minute weekly prison broadcasts.

Prison administrators approved, Fathead and Soupbone took to the airwaves, and the public was delighted. By today's comedy standards, the routines were clean and corny but politically incorrect. In one routine, Fathead and Soupbone did the following dialogue:

Fathead: "They give me life fer just goin' off an leavin' my wife."

Soupbone: "Now wait a minute, Fathead...How did you leave your wife?"

Fathead: "Why, I left her dead!"[1]

Perhaps not cutting-edge humor, but for the 1930s it provided what the Texas public wanted, and appreciated. By the 1940s "Thirty Minutes Behind the Walls" had become a major broadcasting event throughout Texas with the public often attending the live broadcasts done in Huntsville.

"Thirty Minutes Behind the Walls" had become so institutionalized and popular by the 1940s that some electric chair executions were actually postponed or rescheduled so as not to interfere with the weekly radio broadcasts.

In 1946 the following letter was submitted to the Board of Pardons and Paroles in Austin from prison officials in Huntsville:

> The execution of L.C. Newman of Polk County, is set for Thursday, July 18th [1946] and is to take place a few minutes past midnight, Wednesday, July 17th. Our 430th broadcast of "Thirty Minutes Behind the Walls" is scheduled for Wednesday evening, July 17th, at 10:30 [P.M.]. That means just a little more than 1 hour's time will elapse between the ending of the broadcast and the execution of Newman if it is carried out that date.
>
> Last Wednesday evening we had 373 outside visitors in the auditorium for the program, and approximately 40 inmates. We will probably have more than that for the broadcast tomorrow night. We do not have sufficient means to notify the public of any change or cancellation of the program. And too, the "gloom" among the inmates is always "heavy" on execution nights.
>
> In view of the above, we respectfully request your honorable Board to make recommendations to Governor Stevenson that L.C. Newman be granted a 24-hour extension of time so that the program and execution will not conflict.
>
> A precedent will be broken if this request is not granted. In the more than 8 years "Thirty Minutes Behind the Walls" has been on the air several execution dates have been postponed so there would be no conflict in the two.

In making this request we urge you to take immediate actions, so in the event the execution date is not advanced we will have sufficient time to cancel the broadcast from the prison here.

[From the file of L.C. Newman, #277, executed July 19, 1946.][2]

The postponement was granted. Oh, by the way Inmate Newman, you get another twenty-four hours to sit in your death cell and think about Old Sparky. But, on the bright side, you'll get to hear one last broadcast of "Thirty Minutes Behind the Walls."

Ironically one of the most bizarre radio-related incidents in Texas prison history occurred on death row during the early 1930s before "Thirty Minutes Behind the Walls" had begun broadcasting.

Since death cell convicts were confined to their cells twenty-four hours a day, they had far more idle time than the general population inmates, who were expected to work six days a week. One of the ways prison officials helped placate the condemned men and help them pass their remaining time was to play a radio in the death cell. One of the favorite programs was Nashville's "Grand Ole Opry."

In 1931 the death cells held two inmates who were constantly arguing, shouting, threatening, and generally verbally fighting with each other between their cells. One was Joe Shield, who had shot and killed his wife, mother-in-law, and father-in-law from a distance of two hundred yards with a 30-30 rifle. The murders had occurred in the town of Brookesmith less than a year earlier. He claimed that his in-laws had encouraged his wife to take their children and leave him. Shield hoped the governor would commute his sentence for the children's sake.[3]

The other condemned convict, Ira McKee, was a Palo Pinto County farmer convicted of murder. McKee and Shield had both been found guilty of murder and sentenced to death. Both of their respective cases were being appealed, and no definite death date had been set for either of them.

McKee liked to argue and yell, and Shield thought McKee was too loud and obnoxious. McKee thought Shield was arrogant and never missed an opportunity to tell him so. And even though the condemned men were positioned so that several cells were between them, the two argued all day long and often into the night hours. The other convicts on death row grew tired of it, but unable to leave their own cells, there was nothing they could do about the incessant bickering and screaming between McKee and Shield.

Positioning on death row was done by order of execution number. In time McKee and Shield found themselves housed in adjoining death cells. Then the verbal yelling, cussing, screaming, and abuse really started in earnest—much to the chagrin of the other prisoners. Men condemned to death have little to lose, so they really went after each other verbally, and the hatred between them intensified daily.

But on Saturday nights when the Grand Ole Opry came over the radio from Nashville, there was an unspoken truce between them. On one Saturday they decided to write a letter to the Opry to request songs. Shield helped dictate what to say in the letter, while McKee wrote. Shield requested that they play "Eighth of January," while McKee wanted them to play "Black Bottom."

Later, when the two resumed their fighting, McKee said he had requested "Black Bottom" because he knew Shield's bottom would be burned black in the electric chair. Shield countered that his request, "Eighth of January," had been made because that's when McKee would die in the chair.[4] At that point, neither McKee nor Shield had been assigned a definite execution date so Shield's prediction was merely guesswork.

The next Saturday both men were delighted when the announcer at the Opry said he had requests from "two unfortunate men on death row at Huntsville State Prison in Texas." Both "Black Bottom" and "Eighth of January" were then aired.

During the summer of 1931, McKee left Huntsville on a bench warrant for his appeal to his death sentence, hoping to get it overturned or at least reduced to life in prison. On August 14, 1931, Joe Shield was executed in Old Sparky. McKee, away on bench warrant, wasn't on death row to see his enemy have his bottom "burned black." McKee was too busy trying to get his own death sentence reduced.

His appeal was denied, and his own execution was upheld by the appeals court. McKee was returned to death row at Huntsville a desperate, frustrated, out-of-control madman. When he was returned to his death cell, his swearing, screaming, and ranting could be heard throughout the prison yard outside death row. He had gone crazy.

The Saturday night after he returned to Huntsville, the Grand Ole Opry came over the death row radio and the song "Eighth of January" was played. McKee threw things and literally beat his head against the bars of his cell.

The reason for McKee's final plunge off the deep end of sanity? From his grave, with his bottom already black, Shield got the last laugh. He had correctly predicted McKee's death date.

McKee had been sentenced to die in the electric chair on January 8, 1932.[5]

Postscript:

HUNTSVILLE: Jan 8—(AP)—Flickering lamps atop an oaken control board flashed twice here early Friday morning—and the state of Texas had added two more names to the roll of those who have paid for their crimes in the electric chair.

Ira McKee, 32, Palo Pinto county farmer, was the first to die.[6]

Houston Post-Dispatch, January 8, 1932

1   "Texas Prison Rodeo," *New Handbook of Texas in Six Volumes* (Austin: The Texas State Historical Association, 1996)
2   Marquart, *The Rope, The Chair, and the Needle—Capital Punishment in Texas, 1923-1990*, pp. 35-36.
3   Umphrey, *The Meanest Man in Texas*, pg. 78.
4   Ibid., pg. 87.
5   Ibid., pg. 103.
6   "Chair Exacts Lives of Pair For Murders," *Houston Post-Dispatch*, January 8, 1932, front page.

Chapter Seventeen

"She Was... a Bit of a Lady Dog"— Bonnie Parker

She never spent a night in a penitentiary, never "caught the chain bus" to Huntsville or Goree or donned the prison uniform of a Texas convict. At the most, Bonnie Parker spent perhaps two hours on one occasion on Texas prison property, and then she never got out of her automobile.

But no collection of Texas prison stories would be complete without at least some mention of Clyde Barrow's criminal "soul partner." The brief two hours she spent on the edge of the Eastham prison farm in the early morning hours of January 16, 1934, etched forever her name in Texas prison annals.

It was the will of providence and the skill of Frank Hamer that assured she would never process into the Goree women's unit as a Texas inmate. She was certainly on her way to Huntsville, but one of her side trips, in Bienville Parish, Louisiana, put an end to all that.

In just twenty-four years she carved her name into Texas and American history books, but her legacy was infamy and notoriety, not achievement. Still, she managed to define herself on her own terms, and today, over seven decades after her death, she remains a folk hero to many despite her vicious and deadly stint as a criminal.

She is difficult to define. She wrote poetry and saved snapshots of herself with Clyde Barrow—the two often posing in lovers' embraces. She also reportedly walked over to a wounded police officer one Easter Sunday, rolled him over with one foot, raised a sawed-off shotgun, fired two shots, point-blank at the officer's head, and exclaimed, "look-a-there, his head bounced just like a rubber ball."

She helped steal a getaway car and then offered dolls found inside it to some impoverished children they encountered in their escape.

At four-foot-ten and eighty-five pounds, she hardly looked like a future legendary criminal. Even the physical descriptions of her defy consensus: pretty, even beautiful, pixyish, dirty, unsavory, unattractive. She was, and is, hard to define. Former Texas Ranger Frank Hamer once offered his simplified impression of Bonnie Parker: "She was—beggin' your pardon—a bit of a lady dog."[1]

Regardless of one's interpretation of her role in history, there can be no disagreement that her life was one of excitement, violence, and danger. Her short life's journey began on October 1, 1910, with her birth in Rowena, Texas, and ended just twenty-four short years later on a dirt road in rural Louisiana. In between she traveled far and wide and often, and one of her stops was at the Eastham farm one January morning in 1934 when she and Barrow helped their buddy Raymond Hamilton escape from prison.

She has been described as an honor student in school and a girl who had a passion for red clothing. Despite her penchant for writing poetry and romance novels, she quickly became involved with the criminal element hanging around West Dallas during the hard times of the 1920s. She married a violent criminal at age sixteen and was physically abused but remained by his side—working as a waitress to make ends meet. Despite his abuse, she had "Roy and Bonnie" tattooed on her right thigh to commemorate her marriage. The tattoo was one of the positive identifying marks after her death.

While her husband was in prison, she met another criminal named Clyde Barrow in 1930. Only three months after they met, he was jailed and she smuggled a gun into his cell so he could escape.

Barrow, however, was later captured and returned to Texas and sentenced to prison on the Eastham farm. After two years and an act of self-mutilation (he chopped, or had another inmate chop, two toes off to avoid a work detail), he was released in 1932.

Bonnie Parker remained loyal to Barrow during his prison years, and once he was freed she quickly joined him in a crime spree that spanned several state lines and captured newspaper headlines nationally.

In 1932 she was captured and arrested in Kaufman, Texas, for her part in a failed robbery attempt, but a grand jury later no billed her. Reunited with Barrow once again, the two began committing violent crimes in earnest.

They killed two police officers in Atoka, Oklahoma, then gunned down a grocery-store owner in Sherman, Texas, murdered another citizen in Temple, Texas, and killed yet another law officer in Dallas. Later an unarmed town marshal would be gunned down in Arkansas.

A fascinated nation followed their exploits through newspaper coverage that often tried to make them out as modern Robin Hood characters rather than the violent killers they were. But their criminal lifestyle was not a romantic tale of compassionate stealing to give to the poor. And it was not without considerable danger.

In Missouri they barely managed to escape a violent shootout with police. In 1933 Bonnie was severely burned after

their car rolled over an embankment. She escaped another shoot-out in Missouri, but that time both she and Clyde were seriously wounded. She never fully recovered from her wounds and walked with a limp her remaining days.

To the American public they had once seemed invincible—or as popularly stated at the time "untouchable"—in their crime spree, but the burns sustained in the car accident and the gunshot wounds to her legs had taken their toll on Bonnie Parker. Still, they were free and uncaptured and hell-bent to continue their violent criminal behavior.

Then in January of 1934 the two plotted to help one of Barrow's criminal buddies, Raymond Hamilton, escape from the Eastham prison farm. While Bonnie Parker waited in the car in the early morning hours, Clyde helped lay cover fire for

Hamilton and others after the convicts had killed a guard and run off in the confusion. In the early morning fog, Bonnie sounded the car horn to beacon the escaping inmates to their ride to freedom. It was a brief stint in Texas prison history but enough to enter her name into prison history books and folklore tales.

At first glance the Eastham raid and escape appeared to be yet another successful criminal exploit for Parker and Barrow. But in their success, they unleashed the force that was ultimately to be their undoing.

They had previously killed police officers, and in response law agencies throughout Texas, Oklahoma, Arkansas, Missouri, and other states were searching for them with the vengeance only a cop-killer can truly know. Killing a police officer was, and still is today, a capital offence punishable by the death penalty.

But at Eastham, Bonnie Parker and Clyde Barrow participated in something that even Clyde, with his prison experience and savvy, could not have anticipated: the wrath of a prison superintendent sworn to avenge the death of one of his prison guards.

Unknown to them, they had set into motion a revenge pledge they had never before encountered in eluding and escaping from determined and furious police officers. Lee Simmons, the prison director, convinced Governor Miriam Ferguson to rehire a retired Texas Ranger named Frank Hamer to track down and capture—or kill—the two persons he held responsible for the murder of his prison guard. Once this was accomplished and Hamer sworn in, Barrow and Parker had exactly 102 days left to live.

They spent those remaining days in violence. On Easter Sunday of 1934 they opened fire on two police officers at Grapevine, Texas. It was this assault in which Bonnie Parker is reported to have fired a shotgun directly into the skull of one

of the officers on the ground and later commented that his head "bounced like a rubber ball." Within a week they had killed another policeman in Oklahoma, and as subjects of a nationwide manhunt by law officers and the Texas prison system special investigator, they took refuge in the backwoods rural areas of Louisiana.

There can be no question that Bonnie Parker was headed to prison in Texas. Her role in the murders of so many law officers would have guaranteed her a cell on death row and an execution number and date.

But Frank Hamer, operating outside the boundaries of Texas, successfully tracked them down to their hideout in Bienville Parish, and at 9:15 A.M. on May 23, Bonnie Parker and Clyde Barrow were gunned down in a barrage of 167 bullets.

As cautious law officers approached the bullet-riddled car, one policeman opened the passenger side door and Bonnie Parker's blood-soaked body fell from the car. She was holding a machine gun, a sandwich, and a pack of cigarettes.

And she was wearing red clothing.

Despite the viciousness of their crimes and murders, the American and Texas public remained fascinated with Bonnie Parker and Clyde Barrow. After their deaths, the car was taken to Arcadia, Louisiana, and their bodies were later delivered to Dallas. Thousands viewed the mangled bodies, and souvenir hunters attempted to strip the final getaway car. Finally, amid public clamor and hysteria, the bodies were buried in their respective families' burial plots.

After her death Bonnie Parker was denied her dream that she and Clyde Barrow be buried together. But death also denied Bonnie Parker her certain imprisonment in the same prison system she had helped violate by aiding in an escape and the murder of a guard.

She spent time in a Kaufman, Texas jail cell but was cleared and released in a relatively short time. But she never did time in "the big house." Still, her short adult life was spent around ex-convicts: her husband, Roy Thornton, and others like Joe Palmer, Raymond Hamilton, Clyde and Buck Barrow. Through them she must have had some idea of the brutality and despair of serving time in Texas prisons in the 1930s.

Even in death her life is hard to define. Had she lived, would she have become such a household name and, to some, folk hero if she had died in the electric chair? Would she have used her prison days before her execution sitting on her bunk on death row writing her poetry?

Thanks to the skill and perseverance of Frank Hamer and the sworn vengeance of Lee Simmons, Texas will never know the answers to those questions.

But, for a couple of fateful hours on the morning of January 16, 1934, Bonnie Parker, the Rowena, Texas girl who wrote poetry and shot policemen, did time on a Texas prison unit.

And Texas prison history will never be the same because of it.

1   Frost and Jenkins, *"I'm Frank Hamer": The Life of a Texas Peace Officer*, pg. 180.

Chapter Eighteen

"The 1934 Escape From Death Row"—The Only Successful Break

It was a Saturday afternoon, the twenty-first of July in 1934, and old-timers were claiming Texas was in the midst of one of the hottest summers in recent memory. It was, in fact, one of the hottest summers of record, and the Huntsville Walls Unit inmates had turned out in droves to sit in the bleachers of the baseball field and try to pick up some semblance of a breeze as they watched the game.

Over a thousand inmates were thought to be at the game that afternoon—nearly the entire prison unit with the exception of five inmates in the death cells. Four of them were there awaiting execution, and the fifth inmate had been placed there for "protective custody" to keep other inmates from attacking him. The "death sentence" inmates included the infamous members of the Bonnie and Clyde Gang: Raymond Hamilton and Joe Palmer. Two other condemned killers named Blackie Thompson and Ira Rector were also locked up that day. A fifth inmate, Pete McKenzie, well known for killing Chief Detective Sam Street of San Antonio, was in the death cells to protect him for retaliation for stabbing another popular inmate to death in the Walls Unit showers.

Only seven months earlier Clyde Barrow and Bonnie Parker had freed Joe Palmer and Raymond Hamilton from the Eastham Unit in a blaze of gunfire that had killed Major Crowson. They were under particularly close custody inside the death cells. When sentenced to Eastham, Hamilton had boasted "I won't be in here long. Clyde Barrow won't let me lay around a prison farm."

When sentenced to death after being recaptured, he had boasted to *Houston Press* reporter Harry McCormick, "I'll break out of the death house. And when I do, I'll come by to see you."[1] Although Clyde Barrow was now dead and no threat to spring his cousin a second time, prison officials were taking no chances with Hamilton or Palmer.

At least three other inmates were prowling around the lower yard that day, but nobody really paid them much attention in the heat of the mid-afternoon. A few other inmate workers were doing various jobs around the unit, but for the most part the Walls Unit appeared deserted that day.

Unknown to the inmates and most other visitors was the fact that Lee Simmons, the prison director, had been tipped off that morning and had caught some inmates digging a tunnel from beneath the print shop towards the wall. The inmates had been taken into custody and locked into solitary confinement with almost nobody taking notice.

From a convict point of view, the baseball game was a good one. The Huntsville Prison Tigers were leading the semi-pro team from Brenham, Texas, by the score of 5 to 1 going into the ninth inning.

From inside the massive, tall red brick walls that gave the prison its name, nobody could see the two black Ford V-8s drive slowly down Avenue I and park a couple of blocks from the southwest picket tower. Nobody, perhaps, except Officer

Carey Burdeaux, who was manning the tower. But if he noticed the cars, he probably dismissed them as just two more of many cars that passed along Avenue I each day.

Burdeaux's guard post was situated high above the southwest corner of the prison unit in a small boxed-in guard shack that was accessible only by the long, narrow steel ladder leading up the outside of the brick wall from the sidewalk.

As the visiting team, Brenham was batting in the top of the ninth inning. The batter had run the count to three balls and two strikes, and the Prison Tigers pitcher was in his windup when three rapid gunshots erupted from the lower yard.

Despite the intimidating brick walls with their armed guard towers, the Walls Unit had been the scene of several escape attempts. Only recently the infamous escape artist Charlie Frazier had tried twice to go over using a ladder. With the tunnel effectively shut down, most officers and inmates probably assumed it was another ladder attempt that afternoon that prompted the gunshots. Probably more than a few people there suspected Charlie Frazier was somehow involved again.

They were right on both counts. But when the gunfire finally ended, the wounded and dead removed, and the whole escape attempt analyzed, even the veteran prison guards and lifer convicts were amazed.

Joe Palmer, Raymond Hamilton, and Blackie Thompson had escaped from the death cells—something almost nobody would have considered possible to attempt much less accomplish. Last seen, they were speeding north of Huntsville on Highway 75 in the two black Ford V-8s.

With Bonnie and Clyde both dead, all suspicion immediately turned to Charlie Frazier. That Frazier was involved in the escape was a known fact; he had been shot that afternoon during his second attempt to scale the wall and was now in the prison hospital in serious condition. But Frazier hadn't been assigned to the death cells and therefore had no way to get into the area to free Thompson, Palmer, and Hamilton much less attempt to escape over the wall with them.

Frazier was known well in Arkansas, Louisiana, and Texas prison systems because he had escaped from them at least nine times—including the bloody shootout and escape from Louisiana's infamous Angola Prison.

Frazier was now confined to the prison hospital, "not expected to survive,"[2] and refusing to give any information to prison officials. Another inmate, Whitey Walker, was killed by guards, and convict Roy Johnson had been slightly wounded. The seventh inmate, Hub Stanley, quickly gave up and ran for cover and later surrendered without a struggle.

As Texas prison officials began to piece together the intricate details of the "impossible" escape, it became clear that Frazier had been a participant—an active participant—but he was only one of several involved.

Initially, the greatest puzzle was how the six inmates involved in the attempt had gotten possession of three Colt .45 automatic pistols. That took several days, but once that piece of the puzzle was in place, Lee Simmons and other prison officials began to put together the complex parts and figure out exactly what had happened that afternoon.

Several days later Simmons had received a tip that one of his guards had been spending money rather freely in Paris, Texas, just a few days after the break.

After repeatedly questioning the guard and eventually placing him in jail, Simmons got the story:

> On the previous Friday night he had received the three guns from persons whom he still claimed he didn't know. On Saturday he had carried the guns to the east gate, riding in on the local wood wagon. He hid the weapons in the office from which he

supervised the woodyard and the sawmill. That afternoon Hub Stanley took the pistols to the upper yard to hide them where they would be available on Sunday after the lower yard was closed. Charlie Frazier picked up the three automatics there—fully loaded. And that was how the weapons had been supplied for the death-cell break.[3]

That information got the guard an eventual fifteen-year sentence in prison himself and also explained how the sequence of events had unfolded that led to three desperados escaping from the most secure prison cells in Texas.

As suspected, Charlie Frazier had been a key figure in the plot, but surprisingly the idea had not been his. Frazier had been shot and seriously wounded four months earlier trying to scale the walls in Huntsville. While he had been in the hospital that time, he had come into contact with another wounded inmate, Whitey Walker.

Walker and several inmates including Blackie Thompson had escaped from an Oklahoma prison and gone on a two-state crime spree. Captured in Texas, Walker had been wounded and was therefore in the Walls Unit hospital at the same time as Frazier.

Blackie Thompson, in the meantime, was sentenced to death and placed in the Texas death cells at Huntsville. Walker confided to Frazier, the infamous escape artist, that he would like to spring Thompson from the death house. Frazier, of course, never heard an escape plan he didn't consider.

Frazier discovered that one of the guards was heavily in debt and arranged to have money supplied to the guard in return for slipping the three automatic pistols into the prison unit. Frazier was concerned because prison officials were watching him, he needed an inmate trusty to retrieve the guns. That had necessitated the involvement of Hub Stanley, who delivered them to Frazier.

The discovery of the tunnel under the print shop possibly required Frazier, Stanley, and Walker to act sooner than initially planned. Discovery of escape attempts usually result in "lock-downs" in which inmates are locked in their cells indefinitely while prison officials "shake down" the unit looking for contraband, weapons, and escape tools. That would have increased the odds greatly that guards would find the three automatic pistols.

But the fact that the two black Ford V-8s were sitting two blocks away with engines running suggests that the original escape plan was scheduled for Saturday afternoon.

The possibility exists too that Frazier was somehow responsible for Lee Simmons being tipped off about the underground tunnel. By having Simmons preoccupied with that escape attempt, Frazier would have more freedom to implement his own plan. That he would give up other inmates to further his own escape wasn't new for Frazier. After the Angola escape he had sent several fellow escapees to a point on the river where he knew they would be caught, allowing him to slip away during the diversion.

Simmons later recalled that after apprehending the tunneling inmates beneath the print shop, he was escorting them across the yard to solitary when he noticed Charlie Frazier standing by himself. Simmons thought it odd that Frazier was not at the baseball game and even more surprising that he wasn't involved in the tunnel escape attempt but said or did nothing to him as they passed in the yard.

It probably saved his life: Frazier almost certainly was armed with the three automatic Colt .45s at the time.

Late afternoon, during the ninth inning of the ball game, two convict kitchen workers carried evening meals to the men locked in the death cells. Leading them to the building was an inmate trusty named Lee Brazil, who had the keys. Arriving at the gate to the death cells, Brazil unlocked the heavy door and let the two kitchen workers and himself inside. Before he could relock it, Charlie Frazier stepped up and stuck two of the pistols in Brazil's face and demanded he step back.

The trusty did so, and Frazier entered the death house and locked Brazil and the two kitchen workers in one of the empty cells. Since the plan was designed to release Thompson from the death cells, Frazier opened his cell first and released him. He then released Joe Palmer, who convinced him to open the gate to Raymond Hamilton's cell. The other two inmates, Rector and McKenzie, were offered freedom but chose to remain in their cells.

At this point the plan had worked perfectly. The baseball game and tunnel discovery had provided excellent diversions. But soon the ball game would be over and inmates would return to their cells and work stations. Frazier had escaped many times before and knew that timing was critical now.

Frazier, Hamilton, Thompson, and Palmer then moved from the death cells into the yard where they were joined by Whitey Walker, Roy Johnson, and Hub Stanley. Together, they came upon Officer W.G. McConnell and, using their pistols, forced him to join them as a hostage shield.

At the prison machine shop they stole a pair of bolt cutters and then went to the fire station and cut the chain holding one of the extension fire ladders. Carrying the ladder, they went to the west wall that was protected by the guard tower on the southwest corner of the unit. Inside that elevated tower that afternoon was Officer Carey Burdeaux.

Holding their pistols to McConnell's head, they ordered Burdeaux to throw up his hands and keep quiet. Burdeaux did so—an act that Simmons later condemned him for. "Had Burdeaux simply dropped to his knees to fire a single shot in the air, all would have been different," Simmons later wrote.[4]

Given Charlie Frazier's violent nature, however, one of those "differences" Simmons alluded to would have been the assured killing of Officer McConnell.

Frazier had picked the southwest control tower because, once they had reached it on the extension ladder, they could use the outside permanent steel ladder to reach the street outside and the waiting escape cars. With Burdeaux incapacitated, the convicts placed the ladder against the wall, and in a rare show of consideration for someone else, Frazier ordered the death cell escapees up the ladder first. Possibly he wanted to see if they would draw fire.

At the baseball stadium, the game had gone to the top of the ninth inning. At the guard tower, Raymond Hamilton was the first to scale the ladder and enter the booth. He took Burdeaux's pistol as Joe Palmer climbed up. Blackie Thompson was the third to enter the guard shack, and he picked up Burdeaux's rifle.

The three had started down the long steel stairs to the street as Charlie Frazier began climbing up the ladder from inside. The Prison Tigers pitcher wound up to make his three ball and two strike pitch just as Officer Ed Roberts took aim at Charlie Frazier from another control tower to the north of the ladder.

Roberts fired three times, and Frazier fell to the ground. Outside, Thompson ran back up to the picket and joined as Frazier, Johnson, and Walker opened fire on Officer Roberts. The officer held his position and continued returning fire. Soon another officer from east of Burdeaux's station joined in the shooting. When the firing stopped, Frazier lay on the ground with multiple gunshot wounds so serious he wasn't expected to recover. Whitey Walker was shot through the head and killed instantly. Roy Johnson had been wounded, not seriously, and Hub Stanley had run for cover and later surrendered. Officer McConnell, who had been the hostage "shield," also was able to break away during the confusion and was unharmed.

On the other side of the wall, however, Thompson, Palmer, and Hamilton raced down the stairs to the street. At the first sounds of gunshots, the two cars had pulled up to the bottom of the stairs. Two of the escapees jumped in the first car and the third in the second auto. In the process, Raymond Hamilton was grazed on one foot by gunfire.

The cars sped out of Huntsville, and for the second time in barely seven months Raymond Hamilton and Joe Palmer had escaped from a Texas prison in a hail of gunfire. Blackie Thompson had joined them in the first escape from the maximum security Texas death house.

The escape plan had been the design of Whitey Walker with the goal of helping his friend Blackie Thompson escape the death cells. He succeeded, but in the process he lost his own life. Roy Johnson and Hub Stanley were locked up in solitary confinement.

Charlie Frazier miraculously recovered from his wounds as he had so many other gunshots before. As soon as he could be removed from the hospital, he was locked in one of the death cells he had helped open during the escape. Despite Lee Simmon's vehement denials, rumors persist that Frazier was "welded" into his cell and denied medical care and even personal grooming for nearly sixteen months. Simmons later admitted denying Frazier shaving privileges.

But the other three convicts—Raymond Hamilton, Joe Palmer, and Blackie Thompson—were free again and the objects of one of the most massive nationwide manhunts ever staged.

During Thanksgiving of 1998 an inmate named Martin Gurule succeeded in hiding several hours on the roof of Texas Death Row and then scaling a chain link fence and razor wire under heavy rifle fire. He succeeded in getting over the fence and was the subject of a manhunt for several days before being found drowned in the nearby Trinity River.

Gurule's escape from Death Row occurred some sixty-four years after the successful 1934 escape. The fact that he never made it very far from the prison compound doesn't diminish his daring feat of escape, but, in reality, he never achieved freedom from Death Row.

Only Raymond Hamilton, Joe Palmer, and Blackie Thompson can claim that distinction.

And no, history did not record if the pitch was a ball or a strike.

1   Phillips, *Running with Bonnie and Clyde—The Ten Fast Years of Ralph Fults*, pg. 223.
2   "Texas Death Cell Delivery," *Houston Post*, July 24, 1934, pg. 7.
3   Simmons, *Assignment Huntsville*, pp. 155-158.
4   Ibid., pg. 153.

Chapter Nineteen

"Six Blasts of Current"— Joe Palmer and Raymond Hamilton

For the second time in 1934 Raymond Hamilton had made good on boasts that he would break out of prison. Of course, in the process, people were dying to help him become a prophet, but nevertheless he was once again a free man in July of that year.

Hamilton and Joe Palmer captivated the Texas public's attention during 1934 and 1935. In fact, in a violent 1934 that also saw the deaths of Bonnie and Clyde, John Dillinger, and Charles "Pretty Boy" Floyd, the two Texas death house escapees claimed national attention on the same scale.

Probably because of their connections to the Clyde Barrow Gang, Hamilton and Palmer had become celebrity criminals in their own rights. The Eastham prison break in January, orchestrated by Bonnie and Clyde, had made their names household words. Their escape from the Texas death row cells seven months later made them criminal icons in Texas and elsewhere.

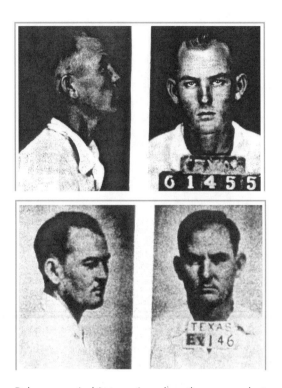

Joe Palmer was in his twenties when the upper photos were taken and thirty-two years old when the lower "execution" mug shot was made. These photos, probably not more than ten years apart, indicate that prison life, the fugitive lifestyle, and shootouts with police and prison officials had aged the notorious criminal quickly.

Almost completely ignored after the sensational July escape was Blackie Thompson—the condemned convict who was the original object of the escape plot. Whitey Walker, who had arranged with Frazier to have the guns sneaked into the Walls Unit, was killed during the escape attempt. After the death cell escape, Thompson had separated from the others and continued his bank robbing independently.

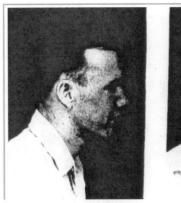

Raymond Hamilton

On December 6, 1934, he was ambushed near Amarillo and escaped, leading officers on a fifteen-mile chase before being forced off the road. In a desperate last stand, Blackie Thompson was killed in the final shoot-out with law officers. He would never return to Huntsville or the Walls Unit death cells.

Only three weeks after the Huntsville escape, Joe Palmer was recaptured in Paducah, Kentucky, when law officers discovered him sleeping on a railroad embankment. Palmer's arrest was simple and nonviolent: The officers kicked the loaded .45 away from his body as he slept and woke him up. He later claimed "The Lord had his arm around those two cops. If I hadn't been dead tired for sleep, you'd have to bury them."[1]

After his arrest Palmer was understandably uncooperative with Paducah police, who could not identify him because Palmer had mutilated his fingerprints by rubbing them on concrete. An anonymous tip to police, however, helped them identify one of the most wanted men in the country and return Joe Palmer to Huntsville.[2]

At Huntsville he was later transferred to Anderson, Texas, on April 6, 1935, and sentenced to death for his involvement

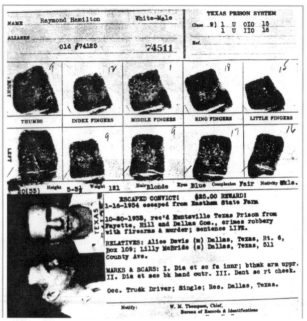

Reward notice for Raymond Hamilton, 1934.

in the death of Major Crowson at Eastham during the Bonnie and Clyde breakout. His execution date was set for May 10, 1935. At that time Palmer, "hate gleaming from his eyes," delivered a tirade and shouldered the blame for the Crowson killing:

> No power on earth could have kept me from killing Crowson. I hated him and meant to kill him if it was the last thing I ever did. Raymond Hamilton was framed and is innocent; he has never killed a man.[3]

It was Raymond Hamilton, however, who had become the focal point of newspaper attention after the deaths of Bonnie Parker and Clyde Barrow. After the death cell escape they had plenty to report for another ten months.

Sometimes working with his brother Floyd and at times working with other criminal acquaintances, Hamilton resumed his bank robbing career and again appeared to be immune from police capture or arrest.

On December 8, 1934, he was involved in the robbery of a Continental Oil Company warehouse near Dallas. In February he and his brother Floyd robbed a bank in Carthage, Texas. That evening, as they visited Dallas to see Raymond's girlfriend, they were ambushed and escaped only after a fierce firefight with Dallas police officers.

Shortly afterward Hamilton was involved in a robbery of a Texas National Guard armory at Beaumont that resulted in the acquisition of several automatic rifles. He then reappeared near McKinney, Texas, where he escaped yet another police shoot-out.

All of these exploits captured the attention of Texans throughout the state during the winter of 1934-35. Hamilton's miraculous escapes from shoot-outs in Dallas and McKinney only added to his already legendary image as a swashbuckling bandit.

Always brash and arrogant, Hamilton sat down after the McKinney shoot-out and wrote a postcard to Texas prison director Lee Simmons.

> You be good to L.C. Barrow, Joe Palmer and Jim _____. Jim is not to blame for himself. I could live in Dallas always and not be bothered. Here is hoping Warden Waid and old Lee Simmons never see me again in that damnable place. Have plenty of Whiskey, jack and women. Dam Huntsville.
> Raymond Hamilton[4]

On March 28, 1935, Hamilton participated in a bank robbery in Prentiss, Mississippi, in which a posse of fifteen officers was disarmed. Later, during the escape, Hamilton was

Joe Palmer and Raymond Hamilton may have been more notorious than Bonnie and Clyde at the time of their executions. This full-page banner headline indicates the almost legendary status they had achieved with their crime sprees and escapes from the Eastham prison farm and later the Texas death house at Huntsville.

involved again in shooting his way out of several traps. From Mississippi he worked his way back to Fort Worth, and on April 5 he was captured in a rail yard.

The desperado and veteran of so many police shoot-outs surrendered peacefully despite the fact he was armed with two automatics at the time of his arrest. The next day he was returned to the prison at Huntsville and Lee Simmons.

On April 8 he was sentenced to die for the murder of Major Crowson, and his execution date was set for May 10. He and Joe Palmer were scheduled to die together. At the time of his sentencing, Hamilton "grinning defiance and hate" delivered an oration in which he declared his innocence of murder. He concluded with the statement "If there are 'hants' [haunts] then I'm coming back and kick the whole bunch out of bed."[5]

But now for the second time, he and Joe Palmer were reunited in Huntsville's famed death house.

Texas justice in 1935 was swift. Inmates in the death cells could not look to endless years of appeals and legal maneuvering to avoid execution. Their date with Old Sparky was only three weeks away.

Despite the interweaving of their lives by design and circumstance, Joe Palmer and Raymond Hamilton had never really been friends. Clyde Barrow's raid on Eastham had been designed to free Hamilton, and Palmer had been allowed to join simply because Hamilton vouched for him as a fearless man with a pistol.

Later, after the Eastham raid, Palmer had called Hamilton a "punk blabbermouth braggart," and only Clyde Barrow's interference had kept Hamilton from shooting Palmer as he slept.[6]

It had always been Hamilton who was the high-profile, swaggering Texas bandit and Palmer who had been the quiet, but deadly, stoic criminal. That pattern continued in the death cells as the men awaited the arrival of May 10.

At least initially the pattern continued.

Hamilton continued his bravado until May 9—bragging that his lawyers would get his execution commuted or that Texas Governor James Allred would somehow save him from Old Sparky.

Lee Simmons, who as prison director had direct contact with Palmer and Hamilton during their last days in the death house, reported that Hamilton became nervous and restless while Palmer seemed to accept his fate without fear or worry.

In the late afternoon of May 9, just a few hours before the scheduled execution after midnight, Palmer and Hamilton were placed in the same cell together—something not usually done in the death cells.

After Hamilton's legal maneuvering had failed, he had become panicky, and Simmons had the two condemned men placed in the same cell so Palmer could calm him down. It seemed to have worked.

The two men shared the same last meal of fried fish, cream gravy, potatoes au gratin, corn O'Brien, sweet pickles, lettuce, stuffed olives, celery, ice cream and chocolate cake, and dewberry cobbler.

Simmons would later report that Palmer talked to Hamilton about dying and afterlife. Both men, as was not unusual in the death house, had embraced religion and had been consulting with prison chaplains. As Palmer calmed Hamilton down, Simmons reported that he "proved himself as a father confessor, chaplain, friend, and Good Samaritan to Raymond in his last hour."[7]

Despite their past differences and the fact that Hamilton had once tried to kill Palmer as he slept, Palmer had tried to shoulder all the blame for Major Crowson's death at Eastham so Hamilton wouldn't be sentenced to death. Now, as the two were about to step into the death chamber where the electric chair was located, Palmer again tried to shield the other convict by offering to go first to the chair since Hamilton appeared on the verge of a nervous breakdown. The warden approved the gesture and Palmer was prepared and dressed first to enter the death chamber.

Dressed in brown clothing with a slit on one pants leg so the electrode could be attached, Palmer told Hamilton "Good-by, old pal. We'll soon be together again." "That's right," Hamilton answered, gulping. "That's right."[8]

Reporters present to witness the execution later wrote that Palmer had a "genuine smile as he walked toward the chair." Then, with the greeting, "Good morning, gentlemen [it was just after midnight], I have prepared a paper to read in here." He thanked one of the priests who had counseled him and wished him a pleasant trip to Ireland. Then he read his statement, which included "I ask God to accept my ignoble death in atonement for my sins."[9]

He then knelt and asked for the blessing of the four priests present. That done, he stood up, laughing, and walked over to Old Sparky and sat down without the assistance or direction of prison security officers.

After the death mask had been placed on his head, three volleys of electrical current were sent into his body. He was pronounced dead at 12:12 A.M.

A priest had remained in the death cell with Hamilton while Palmer was executed. In a semi-joking manner Hamilton complained about the execution garb he had to wear and added, "Where are my suspenders? My hips are so small that my breeches probably will fall off if somebody can't find them." The suspenders were found and given to him.[10]

Four minutes after Palmer's execution, Raymond Hamilton was led into the death chamber and seated. He had finally resigned himself to his fate and seemed to have calmed down. Crossing himself, he recalled Palmer's last words to him. Then, masked and strapped into the electric chair, he too felt the surge of current. The *Houston Post* reported that "suddenly there was a sizzling noise. The dynamo of the chair screeched eerily. Hamilton's body stiffened against the straps; his hands moved and then slowly closed toward him. Twice more the current seared through his body before he was pronounced dead by the prison physician."[11] The time was precisely 12:27 A.M.

At last the Clyde Barrow Gang had been silenced—"liquidated" as Lee Simmons later claimed—and the two final notorious Texas gangsters had met their execution date. Finally the Eastham and death cell escapes and resulting killings had been avenged by the state.

The executions of such infamous criminals had a profound effect on the other inmates at the Walls Unit. Palmer, in particular, had gained their admiration for his resistance to authority and his willingness to shoulder the blame for the killing of Crowson. Afraid that the two executed men might end up in the indigent "Peckerwood Hill" convict cemetery outside Huntsville, the inmates had collected about fifty dollars to help the families defray the costs of burials in outside cemeteries.

Raymond Hamilton's mother arranged to have him buried in Dallas despite the fact his father had attempted to have him interred in Shreveport.

Joe Palmer was buried in an unmarked grave in a southside San Antonio cemetery beside his mother. Some sixty years later, family members placed a simple marker on his grave that included his full name and the date of his birth, September 29, 1902, and of his death, May 10, 1935.

Joe Palmer and Raymond Hamilton had lived short but violent and criminal lives. Despite the efforts of prison officials to incarcerate them and law officers to ambush them, they had seemingly always found a way out of their predicaments.

Their luck ran out on May 10, 1935, when "six blasts of current—three for each man—silenced forever the one-time bitter tongue of Palmer, and wiped away the grin that Hamilton wore as he went to his death."[12]

1   Simmons, *Assignment Huntsville*, pg. 159.
2   Phillips, *Running With Bonnie and Clyde*, pg. 231.
3   "Hamilton and Palmer Are Electrocuted," *Houston Post*, May 10, 1935, pg. 10.
4   Simmons, pg. 160.
5   "Hamilton and Palmer Are Electrocuted," *Houston Post*, May 10, 1935, pg. 10.
6   Simmons, pg. 167.
7   Ibid., pg. 161.
8   "Hamilton Loses Final Appeal," *Houston Chronicle*, May 10, 1935, pg. 21.
9   "Hamilton and Palmer Are Electrocuted," *Houston Post*, May 10, 1935, pg. 10
10 Hamilton Loses Final Appeal," *Houston Chronicle*, May 10, 1935, pg. 21.
11 "Hamilton and Palmer Are Electrocuted," *Houston Post*, May 10, 1935, pg. 10.
12 Ibid., front page.

Chapter Twenty

"Catchin' the Chain"—Bud Russell

Few men, if any, ever understood Texas convicts better than Bud Russell. From 1905 to 1944 he personally handcuffed *at least* 115,000 prisoners and delivered them to the gates of the Huntsville unit.

Bud Russell, you see, was the transfer agent for the Texas prison system and as such was responsible for picking up convicted felons from Texas county jails and delivering them safely to Huntsville. Nearly 4,000 of his "wards" were escaped convicts being held in other states.

In the conduct of his job, he became a sort of folk hero around the state. From large cities to the smallest, most remote county jails, "Uncle Bud" and his "One-Way Wagon" were recognized instantly.

In many communities, crowds gathered automatically at the site of his custom-built prison wagon for a glimpse of the chained and shackled inmates he was collecting or, in many cases, just to see and photograph the legendary man himself.

From 1922 until his retirement in 1944, it's estimated he drove over 3.9 million miles collecting inmates from 254 Texas counties, 45 states, plus convicts from Mexico and Canada. Of the 115,000 inmates he transported, only one ever escaped, and that was because Russell chose not to kill him.

Russell was born in 1875 on his father's ranch outside Blum, Texas, and grew up around horses, cattle, and cowboys. As a youth he worked a couple of years on the famous Matador Ranch and then served as a constable for five years. His ranch work gave him experience in judging men, and his law enforcement experience gave him background in handling them.

The Texas prison system, then, was the perfect job for him when he hired on with the state in 1905. By 1908 he had advanced to the position of assistant transfer agent, and when his boss left in 1912, Bud Russell became the chief (and only) transfer agent for the prison system. It was a job he would hold until his retirement in 1944.

In the early years he traveled around the state by train, collecting inmates and loading them up—as many as eighty at a time—and escorting them from the far corners of Texas to the east-central prison headquarters in Huntsville. On layovers or train changes he would single-handedly remove the prisoners from the train car and escort them, chained together, down the street to the local jail. He never lost a prisoner, and his legend was already beginning to grow.

In 1922 he stopped shipping inmates by train and started using a transport truck. Occasionally he would escort convicted prisoners back to their county of conviction for court reviews or additional charges, but he was always there again to pick them up and return them to Huntsville. In the end they always returned to prison—hence the name "One-Way Wagon."

The truck was an oversized flatbed truck with a frame of boilerplate and heavy wire mesh. The back was essentially a heavy-gauge metal "cage" with one entrance, consisting of two narrow double doors, at the rear on the driver side. It was the only way in and out for the prisoners being transported.

This 1934 photo shows Bud Russell (right) with the infamous "One-Way Wagon" also known as the "chain bus." (photo courtesy of Texas Prison Museum, Huntsville, Texas)

The inmates, chained together with a short chain around their necks and attached to a longer chain running across one of their shoulders, could not break and run because they were attached to the other prisoners. They also each wore handcuffs.

Inside, the back of the transport wagon had a large steel rod down the center. When a convict entered the back doors, one of his handcuffs was removed and slipped over the steel rod. When the last inmate was inside, the end of the rod had a piece of metal padlocked on the end to prevent any of the handcuffs from being removed from the steel rod. The doors where then double-padlocked with heavy-duty Yale locks. This way he could effectively transport up to thirty inmates at a time.

The very act of being transported in the One-Way Wagon created what has become Texas prison legend. Even today as an inmate boards a prison bus for transfer, he is referred to by inmates and guards alike as being "on the chain." The busses themselves, although radically different today, are still referred to as "chain busses."

The original One-Way Wagon, custom built on an oversized flatbed truck, had heavy-duty springs and a high-performance engine. Aware that he was vulnerable on rural roads and highways, Russell wanted to make sure he wasn't the victim of some inmate's friend or family trying to run him off the road in an escape attempt.

He used thick-tread mud grip tires and once bragged that he could drive the truck 223,000 miles on two sets of tires. Dining fare on the One-Way Wagon couldn't have been too good, either. Russell also claimed to have spent nine cents a meal on convicts during the early days.

The One-Way Wagon really brought Bud Russell into the public eye and made him a well-known legend throughout Texas from the 1920s through the forties.

Among inmates he was so well known that his very name became synonymous with prison life. Just as "Uncle Sam" has become an expression for the United States government, "Uncle Bud" during those years was analogous with the Texas prison system. Inmates ate "Uncle Bud's" chow in the mess halls and picked "Uncle Bud's" cotton in the fields.

In his miles around the state, he picked up and transported, at one time or another, almost every desperate criminal the Texas law officers could arrest and convict.

Clyde Barrow rode the One-Way Wagon on several occasions as did other members of his "gang" including Raymond Hamilton and Joe Palmer. Bud Russell collected—and delivered—the toughest criminals Texas could convict. Always dressed in a suit with a Stetson hat and dark glasses, he presented a pretty formidable figure himself. The pistol and shotgun he always carried helped shore up his authority.

"Uncle Bud" Russell, with shotgun, watches another load of inmates enter the Walls Unit at Huntsville. (photo courtesy of Texas Prison Museum, Huntsville, Texas)

Invariably a prisoner would try to challenge him. One of his favorite responses became, "You were born forty years too late to be tougher than me!"

He later claimed he could "sense" when trouble was brewing, and a few choice words would usually be enough to nip it in the bud. Of the estimated 115,000 inmates he transported, only one ever succeeded in escaping from him. And that was because Russell chose to let him go.

In 1932 he was escorting a small Mexican inmate named Carlos Brazil from El Paso. The One-Way Wagon stopped at the Taylor County jail in Abilene at the end of the day, and Russell was unloading the prisoners for their overnight stay. Brazil had somehow managed to unlock his neck chain and was therefore separated from the other convicts inside the bus. As he exited the door and his handcuff was removed from the steel bar, he bolted for freedom.

Russell, who was a certifiable sharpshooter, chose not to kill him and instead shot him in one foot. Brazil limped into a congregation of churchgoers, and Russell, forced to remain with the other convicts, would not shoot near the crowd for fear of hitting an innocent bystander. His decision to shoot to wound rather than kill resulted in the only escape he ever suffered in thirty-nine years with the prison system.

Russell was so staggered by this affront to his "reputation" he wired this telegram from Abilene:

Abilene, Texas

Lee Simmons
General Manager
Texas Prison System
Huntsville, Texas

Have lost my first prisoner. Am tendering my resignation.

Bud Russell
Transfer Agent[1]

Simmons later recalled that while he realized Russell was dead serious about resigning over the incident, he was not about to lose the best transfer agent the prison system had ever had.

Fashioning a "fake" telegram response, Simmons wrote:

Bud Russell
Transfer Agent

Refuse to accept your resignation. Prefer to discharge you. Please go to hell.

Lee Simmons
General Manager

Simmons left the fake telegram where Russell was sure to find it when he reported to Huntsville with the rest of the El

Paso prisoners. Russell decided to remain with the prison system and left for another run out to West Texas.

As usual crowds at every stop immediately surrounded him, and a local newspaperman asked him about the Brazil escape. Russell showed him the telegram, still thinking it was real, and copies were soon splashed over headlines throughout Texas.

The escape, in the end, only added to his already legendary status. The public, it turned out, also admired his decision not to shoot into a group of innocent bystanders.

Within a month Brazil had been recaptured along the Rio Grande by border guards, and "Uncle Bud" showed up with his One-Way Wagon to escort him to Huntsville. This time the inmate arrived as scheduled.

Bud Russell never killed an inmate in his nearly forty years of service. He intentionally shot Brazil in the foot rather than kill him. On another occasion he thwarted an escape attempt by shooting and creasing the convict on the temple. Like Brazil, the inmate lived to serve time at Huntsville.

The 1930s were hard times for the Texas prison system— for convict and officials alike. Rife with rumors and charges of corruption and brutality, the Texas prison system had been under fire for years when Lee Simmons took over as general manager.

Simmons today is remembered as one of the greatest administrators the prison system has ever employed, but even he was never able to completely eliminate the whispers and charges of corruption and abuse of inmates during his term. He was, however, the consummate public relations government official of his day.

To portray the prison system in a better light to the public, he devised a number of high-profile programs. His most famous and endearing legacy to the system was probably the establishment of the Texas Prison Rodeo. He also developed rudimentary literacy programs and expanded the library systems on the units. A particularly popular program attributed to him was the establishment of a Negro Cotton Picker's Glee Club that traveled around the state, performing in such places as the Rice Hotel in Houston and at Baylor University.

He also promoted sports teams, and the great showdown between the Huntsville Prison Tigers and the Brenham Sun Oilers at Houston's Buff Stadium was his idea.

All of these projects succeeded greatly in improving the prison system's image in the eyes of the public. But they were also often extremely risky since many of them required transporting often-dangerous convicted felons to "free-world" functions and assuring they return back to prison without incident.

To achieve this, Simmons turned repeatedly to "Uncle Bud" Russell and his One-Way Wagon. Not only were the Prison Tigers and the prison orchestra escorted to Buff Stadium for the double-header, the inmates were afterwards taken to Kelly's Restaurant—one of the best in Houston at the time. Uncle Bud then took them back home to Huntsville at the end of a very unusual day.

But beforehand he had driven down to Houston, walked the perimeter of the stadium, checked the exits and seating at the restaurant, and coordinated routes. When the hot, tired, dirty but well-fed ball team and orchestra players made it back to their prison bunks that night, they knew they had been well guarded every minute of that long day by Uncle Bud.

He was married and had a son named Roy, who in later years assisted his dad in the transportation of inmates. Bud Russell also escorted female prisoners from time to time, and on those trips he always took his wife, Minnie, along. That way he never had to worry about his reputation.

Lee Simmons, in his memoirs, relates a story about Minnie Russell on one of the trips in the early years when Bud was

"Uncle Bud" Russell resigning his position as Transfer Agent in 1944. During his thirty-nine-year career it is estimated he transported over 115,000 Texas inmates around the state with only one escape. (photo courtesy of Texas Prison Museum, Huntsville, Texas)

escorting prisoners by train. On this particular trip he was escorting five female prisoners and had to change trains in Houston—requiring an overnight stay at the Harris County jail.

With his wife in the group, he marched the women up to the jailer inside the jail, who instructed them to stand to one side. The inmates complied, but Russell's wife remained standing by herself. The jailer looked at Uncle Bud, who indicated he had never seen her until he had picked her up on this trip.

The jailer barked at Minnie to "get with the rest," and she refused. By Simmons' account the situation was getting pretty tense before Bud Russell admitted, "That's my wife." The records do not indicate if Bud Russell also slept at the Harris County jail that night or not.

On May 28, 1944, he retired to go back to Blum, Texas. He had served the Texas prison system for thirty-nine years and nineteen days. His travels—on trains and in the One-Way Wagon—during those years were the equivalent of fifteen trips around the world.

In Texas he was a legend, but his travels had taken him to forty-five other states, and his reputation and fame had spread beyond the Lone Star State. Upon his retirement, the Associated Press reported that Russell "quits one of the toughest jobs of them all, still with his humor intact, and with ill will toward none—not even the prisoners who gave him trouble."

He died in 1955, his reputation intact. Known by inmates and prison officials alike as a fair and reasonable man, he nevertheless also enjoyed a reputation for toughness when the occasion demanded it.

And still today "chain busses" crisscross Texas highways, and in hundreds of county jails convicted felons sit and wait to "catch the chain."

Many quotes have been attributed to Uncle Bud Russell, but one particularly stands out and defines the man who drove the One-Way Wagon: "You were born forty years too late to be tougher than me."

---

1   Simmons, Lee, *Assignment Huntsville,* pg. 180.

Epilogue

Singin' a Lonesome Song spans a hundred-year period generally from 1863 when Union prisoners salvaged lumber at the Huntsville Unit for Sam Houston's casket until 1963 when Candy Barr walked away from the Goree Unit.

That century represents some of the most colorful—and sometimes most deadly—prisoners to be found anywhere in American prison history.

Ironically the Republic of Texas never got around to building a prison. With statehood, Texas counties were initially given the responsibility of incarcerating convicted felons. The first prison in Texas was the "Walls Unit" at Huntsville—built in 1849 with original walls fifteen feet high and made of sandbrick. The designer of the original prison at Huntsville was Abner H. Cook, and the master brick mason was Captain James Gillaspie.[1]

When overcrowding became a problem at Huntsville, the solution was to lease convicts out to private enterprise rather than raise taxes to build another prison unit. The first lease was issued to railroads in 1867.

It was only a stopgap measure, and the Rusk Penitentiary was built between 1877 and 1883. Designed as an industrial prison to generate revenues for Texas through iron smelting, it was never really successful financially, but in its heyday it actually was bigger, more modern, and more profitable than the Huntsville Unit. However, by 1918, it had ceased to serve as a penitentiary.

By then the convict-leasing program had been expanded from private industry to plantation farming. Some of those plantations were eventually purchased by the state and respresent some of the oldest units in Texas outside of Huntsville. The Ramsey and Retrieve Units near Angleton, the Central Unit south of Sugarland, and the Eastham Unit near Trinity represent only some of the old vestiges of the leasing system.

These tough, mean farm units and the large units at Huntsville and Rusk provide the basis for almost all the stories from *Singin' a Lonesome Song*. They were prison units that spawned tough, violent, and colorful prisoners during the century covered in the book.

But the twenty stories here represent only a tiny fraction of the thousands of stories that passed through prison gates in Texas between 1863 and 1963. The nameless graves lined up in Peckerwood Hill probably would contain enough stories to fill an encyclopedia of crime. Among some of the stories not covered in *Singin' a Lonesome Song* are these:

- The first female inmate convicted in Texas was sentenced to one year for infanticide in 1854.

- The youngest inmate of record was a nine-year-old boy sentenced for robbery in 1884.

- The youngest female inmate was an eleven-year-old girl sentenced that same year for administering poison.

- The most unusual occupation listed by an inmate was "Gentleman Loafer."

- The most unusual disciplinary offense an inmate could be punished for was "worthlessness."

- The shortest sentence on record was for one hour for a Dallas man on November 15, 1870.[2]

As Texas prisons move into the new millenium, the very act of incarcerating human beings will continue to generate controversy and dominate newspaper headlines. It is certain that some kind of controversy surrounded that very first unfortunate inmate who was processed into the Huntsville unit in 1849.

But those who have followed have written their own history and, in the process, contributed to *Singin' a Lonesome Song*.

Inmate work crew on one of the Texas Department of Corrections farm units circa 1950. These isolated units historically produced the most colorfull—and violent—inmates in Texas's prison history. (photo source: Texas State Archives, courtesy of Jester III Unit, Texas Department of Criminal Justice).

1   "Tours to Explore Huntsville, Texas—Prison Driving Tour," A publication of the Huntsville Tourism Council Huntsvile/Walker County Chamber of Commerce, November 1999.

2   Ibid.

Bibliography

Books

Abernethy, Francis Edward, ed. *Legendary Ladies of Texas* (Dallas: E-Heart Press, 1981).

Cotner, Robert C. *The Texas State Capitol* (Austin: The Pemberton Press, 1968).

Frost, H. Gordon and John Jenkins. *"I'm Frank Hamer": The Life of a Texas Peace Officer* (Austin: Pemberton Press, 1968).

Hardin, John Wesley. *The Life of John Wesley Hardin As Written by Himself* (Seguin, Texas: Smith and Moore, 1896). Reprinted in 1961 by the University of Oklahoma Press.

Marquart, James W., et al. *The Rope, the Chair, and the Needle: Capital Punishment in Texas 1923-1990* (Austin: University of Texas Press, 1994).

Metz, Leon. *John Wesley Hardin, Dark Angel of Texas* (El Paso: Mangan Books, 1966).

New Handbook of Texas in Six Volumes (Austin: The Texas State Historical Association, 1996).

Paredes, Americo. *With A Pistol in His Hand* (Austin: University of Texas Press, 1958).

Paulissen, May Nelson and Carl McQueary. *Miriam: The Southern Belle Who Became the First Woman Governor of Texas* (Austin: Eakin Press, 1995).

Phillips, John Neal. *Running with Bonnie and Clyde: The Ten Fast Years of Ralph Fults* (Norman and London: University of Oklahoma Press, 1996).

Simmons, Lee. *Assignment Huntsville: Memoirs of a Texas Prison Official* (Austin: University of Texas Press, 1959).

Umphrey, Don. *The Meanest Man in Texas* (New York: Thomas Nelson Publishers, 1984).

Walker, Donald R. *Penology for Profit: A History of the Texas Prison System 1867-1912* (College Station: Texas A&M University Press, 1988).

Webb, Walter Prescott. *The Texas Rangers: A Century of Frontier Defense* (Austin: The University of Texas Press, 1935).

Newspaper Articles
(With chapter citations)

Angleton Times, March 3, 1933 (Chapter Nine)

Angleton Times, May 31, 1935 (Chapter Nine)

Angleton Times, July 26, 1935 (Chapter Nine)

Austin Statesman, December 10, 1885 (Chapter Four)

Austin Statesman, January 31, 1886 (Chapter Four)

Austin Statesman, July 19, 1913 (Chapter Eleven)

Brownsville Daily Herald, January 4, 1905 (Chapter Eleven)

Houston Chronicle, July 19, 1913 (Chapter Eleven)

Houston Chronicle, May 10, 1935 (Chapter Nineteen)

Houston Chronicle, September 5, 1935 (Chapter Seven)

Houston Chronicle, September 8, 1935 (Chapter Seven)

Houston Chronicle, April 2, 1963 (Chapter Five)

Houston Chronicle, July 7, 1963 (Chapter Eight)

Houston Post, January 2, 1905 (Chapter Eleven)

Houston Post, July 24, 1934 (Chapter Eighteen)

Houston Post, May 10, 1935 (Chapter Nineteen)

Houston Post, August 18, 1935 (Chapter Seven)

Houston Post, August 22, 1935 (Chapter Seven)

Houston Post, September 3, 1935 (Chapter Seven)

Houston Post, September 4, 1935 (Chapter Seven)

Houston Post, September 8, 1935 (Chapter Seven)

Houston Post, October 3, 1960 (Chapter Five)

Houston Post-Dispatch, January 8, 1932 (Chapter Sixteen)

San Antonio Express, January 2, 1905 (Chapter Eleven)

Magazine Articles
(With chapter citations)

Oui Magazine, June 1976 (Chapter Five)

Playboy Magazine, December 1999 (Chapter Five)

Texas Monthly, December 1999 (Chapter Five)

Texas Parade, Vol. 35, No. 5, October 1974 (Chapter Ten)

Vertical Files

Brazoria County Historical Museum, Angleton, Texas

Eugene C. Barker Texas History Collections, University of Texas at Austin

Texas State Library and Archives

Phamplets

43rd Annual Texas Prison Rodeo, Official Souvenir Program, Texas Department of Corrections, Huntsville, Texas, 1974

"Tours to Explore Huntsville, Texas—Prison Driving Tour," a Publication of the Huntsville Tourism Council Huntsville/ Walker County Chamber of Commerce, November 1999.

Index

Index

Other books from

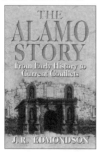

Republic of Texas Press